Learning SciPy for Numerical and Scientific Computing

A practical tutorial that guarantees fast, accurate, and easy-to-code solutions to your numerical and scientific computing problems with the power of SciPy and Python

Francisco J. Blanco-Silva

[PACKT] open source
PUBLISHING   community experience distilled

BIRMINGHAM - MUMBAI

Learning SciPy for Numerical and Scientific Computing

First published: February 2013

Production Reference: 1130213

Published by Packt Publishing Ltd.
Livery Place
35 Livery Street
Birmingham B3 2PB, UK.

ISBN 978-1-78216-162-2

www.packtpub.com

Cover Image by Asher Wishkerman (wishkerman@hotmail.com)

Credits

Author
Francisco J. Blanco-Silva

Reviewers
Lorenzo Bolla

Seth Brown

Ryan R. Rosario

Acquisition Editor
Kartikey Pandey

Commissioning Editor
Maria D'souza

Technical Editor
Devdutt Kulkarni

Project Coordinator
Amigya Khurana

Proofreader
Lesley Harrison

Indexers
Monica Ajmera Mehta

Tejal Soni

Graphics
Aditi Gajjar

Production Coordinator
Nitesh Thakur

Cover Work
Nitesh Thakur

About the Author

Francisco J. Blanco-Silva is the owner of a scientific consulting company — Tizona Scientific Solutions — and adjunct faculty in the Department of Mathematics of the University of South Carolina. He obtained his formal training as an applied mathematician at Purdue University. He enjoys problem solving, learning, and teaching. Being an avid programmer and blogger, when it comes to writing, he relishes finding that common denominator among his passions and skills and making it available to everyone.

He coauthored Chapter 5 of the book *Modeling Nanoscale Imaging in Electron Microscopy, Springer* by Peter Binev, Wolfgang Dahmen, and Thomas Vogt.

This book, as all my other professional endeavors, would have not been possible without the inspiration and teachings of Bradley J. Lucier and Rodrigo Bañuelos, with whom I will be eternally grateful. I would like to send special thanks to my editors, Maria D'souza and Amigya Khurana, for all their patience, help, and expertise. Many colleagues and friends have helped me shape this monograph and encouraged me to get it done (unknowingly or otherwise!): Thierry Zell, Yalçin Sarol, Manfred Stoll, Ralph Howard, Éva Czabarka, Aaron Dutle, Stacey Levine, Alison Malcolm, Scott MacLachlan, and Antoine Flattot, among many others. But the most special thanks goes to my amazing wife, Kaitlin, for all her love, support, encouragement, and willingness to deal with my working for endless hours.

About the Reviewers

Lorenzo Bolla is a Software Architect working in London. He received a PhD in numerical methods applied to engineering problems. His focus is now on high performance web applications, machine-learning algorithms, and any other sort of number crunching he can put his hands on.

He is interested in multiple programming languages and paradigms, cooking, and chess.

Seth Brown is a Data Scientist, trained as a Bioinformatician, with a PhD in computational genomics and biostatistics. He has been using the Python programming language and SciPy since 2006. He discusses his work, data analysis, and Python on his blog – `drbunsen.org`.

Ryan R. Rosario is a Doctoral Candidate at the University of California, Los Angeles. He works in industry as a Data Scientist and he enjoys turning large quantities of massive, messy data into gold. Ryan is heavily involved in the open-source community particularly with R, Python, Hadoop, and machine learning. He has also contributed code to various Python and R projects. Ryan maintains a blog dedicated to data science and related topics at `http://www.bytemining.com`.

Ryan also served as a technical reviewer for the book *NumPy 1.5 Beginner's Guide*, *Ivan Idris, Packt Publishing*.

www.PacktPub.com

Support files, eBooks, discount offers and more

You might want to visit www.PacktPub.com for support files and downloads related to your book.

Did you know that Packt offers eBook versions of every book published, with PDF and ePub files available? You can upgrade to the eBook version at www.PacktPub.com and as a print book customer, you are entitled to a discount on the eBook copy. Get in touch with us at service@packtpub.com for more details.

At www.PacktPub.com, you can also read a collection of free technical articles, sign up for a range of free newsletters and receive exclusive discounts and offers on Packt books and eBooks.

http://PacktLib.PacktPub.com

Do you need instant solutions to your IT questions? PacktLib is Packt's online digital book library. Here, you can access, read and search across Packt's entire library of books.

Why Subscribe?

- Fully searchable across every book published by Packt
- Copy and paste, print and bookmark content
- On demand and accessible via web browser

Free Access for Packt account holders

If you have an account with Packt at www.PacktPub.com, you can use this to access PacktLib today and view nine entirely free books. Simply use your login credentials for immediate access.

Table of Contents

Preface   **1**

Chapter 1: Introduction to SciPy   **5**
  What is SciPy?   **5**
  How to install SciPy   **8**
  SciPy organization   **10**
  How to find documentation   **13**
  Scientific visualization   **16**
  Summary   **17**

Chapter 2: Top-level SciPy   **19**
  Object essentials   **20**
    Datatype   21
    Indexing   22
  The array object   **24**
  Array routines   **26**
    Routines for array creation   26
    Routines for the combination of two or more arrays   32
    Routines for array manipulation   34
    Routines to extract information from arrays   35
  Summary   **37**

Chapter 3: SciPy for Linear Algebra   **39**
  Matrix creation   **39**
  Matrix methods   **44**
    Operations between matrices   44
    Functions on matrices   45
    Eigenvalue problems and matrix decompositions 47
    Image compression via the singular value decomposition   48
    Solvers   49
  Summary   **51**

Chapter 4: SciPy for Numerical Analysis — 53

Evaluation of special functions — 53
Convenience and test functions — 53
Univariate polynomials — 54
The gamma function — 56
The Riemann zeta function — 57
Airy (and Bairy) functions — 58
Bessel and Struve functions — 59
Other special functions — 60

Interpolation and regression — 60

Optimization — 68
Minimization — 68
Roots — 69

Integration — 72
Exponential/logarithm integrals — 72
Trigonometric and hyperbolic trigonometric integrals — 73
Elliptic integrals — 73
Gamma and beta integrals — 74
Numerical integration — 74

Ordinary differential equations — 75

Lorenz Attractors — 77

Summary — 80

Chapter 5: SciPy for Signal Processing — 81

Discrete Fourier Transforms — 81

Signal construction — 83

Filters — 85
LTI system theory — 88
Filter design — 88
Window functions — 88
Image interpolation — 90
Morphology — 92

Summary — 93

Chapter 6: SciPy for Data Mining — 95

Descriptive statistics — 95
Distributions — 96
Interval estimation, correlation measures, and statistical tests — 97
Distribution fitting — 100

Distances — 101

Clustering — 105
Vector quantization and k-means — 105

Hierarchical clustering	107
Summary	**110**
Chapter 7: SciPy for Computational Geometry	**111**
Structural model of oxides	113
A finite element solver for Poisson's equation	117
Summary	**121**
Chapter 8: Interaction with Other Languages	**123**
Fortran	**123**
C/C++	**125**
Matlab/Octave	**127**
Summary	**129**
Index	**131**

Preface

SciPy has been an integral part of the computational environment of choice of many scientists for years. One of the challenges of our trade is to bring to a single workstation the production of professionals with different visions, techniques, tools, and software (from the pure mathematician, to the hardcore engineer).

We are required to produce scripts in which, for example, there are combinations of experiments written and performed in SciPy itself, C/C++, Fortran, R, or MATLAB®. We often receive extremely large amounts of raw data from some signal acquisition device. From all this heterogeneous material, we employ SciPy to retrieve this data, manipulate it, experiment it, analyze it, and once finished with the analysis, produce high-quality documentation with professional-looking diagrams and visualizations aids.

SciPy is the perfect way to coordinate everything in a smooth, reliable, and coherent way. It allows performing all these tasks with ease. This is partly because many dedicated software tools easily extend the core features of SciPy, and interfacing with non-Python-based packages and software is extremely easy.

In summary this book presents the most robust programming environment to date. We will show you how to use this system from basic training of manipulation of data, to a very detailed exposition through examples of state-of-the-art research in different branches of science and engineering.

What this book covers

Chapter 1, Introduction to SciPy, shows the benefits of using the combination of Python, NumPy, SciPy, and matplotlib as a programming environment for scientific purposes. We will learn how to install it, explore the environment, use it for some quick computations, and figure out a few good ways to search for help.

Chapter 2, Top-level SciPy, explores in depth the creation and basic manipulation of the object array used by SciPy, as an overview of the NumPy libraries.

Chapter 3, SciPy for Linear Algebra, covers applications of SciPy to applications with large matrices, including solving systems or computation of eigenvalues and eigenvectors.

Chapter 4, SciPy for Numerical Analysis, is without a doubt one of the most interesting chapters in this book. It covers with great detail the definition and manipulation of functions (one or several variables), the extraction of their roots, extreme values (optimization), computation of derivatives, integration, interpolation, regression, and applications to the solution of ordinary differential equations.

Chapter 5, SciPy for Signal Processing, explores construction, acquisition, quality improvement, compression, and feature extraction of signals (in any dimension). It is covered with beautiful and interesting examples from the field of image processing.

Chapter 6, SciPy for Data Mining, covers applications of SciPy for collection, organization, analysis, and interpretation of data, with examples taken from statistics and clustering.

Chapter 7, SciPy for Computational Geometry, explores the construction of triangulation of points, convex hulls, Voronoi diagrams, and many applications. At this point in the book, it will be possible to combine techniques from all the previous chapters to show state-of-the-art research performed with ease with SciPy, and we will explore a few good examples from Material Sciences and Experimental Physics.

Chapter 8, Interaction with Other Languages, introduces one of the main strengths of SciPy – the ability to interact with other languages such as C/C++, Fortran, R, and MATLAB®/Octave.

What you need for this book

To work with the examples and try out the code in this book, all you need is a recent build of Python (2.7 or higher), with the libraries NumPy, SciPy, and matplotlib. Recipes to install all these are provided throughout the book.

Who this book is for

This book is for scientists, engineers, programmers, or analysts with knowledge of Python. For some of the sections, a decent command over linear algebra, calculus, and some statistics is needed to understand some of the concepts, but otherwise this book is mostly self contained.

Conventions

In this book, you will find a number of styles of text that distinguish between different kinds of information. Here are some examples of these styles, and an explanation of their meaning.

Code words in text are shown as follows: "Within a terminal session, change directories to the folder where the NumPy libraries are stored, that contains the setup.py file."

A block of code is set as follows:

```
import numpy
import matplotlib.pyplot
x=numpy.linspace(0,numpy.pi,32)
fig=matplotlib.pyplot.figure()
fig.plot(x, numpy.sin(x))
fig.savefig('sine.png')
```

Any command-line input or output is written as follows:

```
% python setup.py build -fcompiler=<compiler>
```

New terms and **important words** are shown in bold.

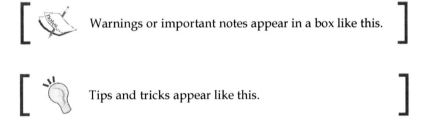

> Warnings or important notes appear in a box like this.

> Tips and tricks appear like this.

Reader feedback

Feedback from our readers is always welcome. Let us know what you think about this book—what you liked or may have disliked. Reader feedback is important for us to develop titles that you really get the most out of.

To send us general feedback, simply send an e-mail to feedback@packtpub.com, and mention the book title via the subject of your message.

If there is a topic that you have expertise in and you are interested in either writing or contributing to a book, see our author guide on www.packtpub.com/authors.

Customer support

Now that you are the proud owner of a Packt book, we have a number of things to help you to get the most from your purchase.

Errata

Although we have taken every care to ensure the accuracy of our content, mistakes do happen. If you find a mistake in one of our books—maybe a mistake in the text or the code—we would be grateful if you would report this to us. By doing so, you can save other readers from frustration and help us improve subsequent versions of this book. If you find any errata, please report them by visiting http://www.packtpub.com/submit-errata, selecting your book, clicking on the **errata submission form** link, and entering the details of your errata. Once your errata are verified, your submission will be accepted and the errata will be uploaded on our website, or added to any list of existing errata, under the Errata section of that title. Any existing errata can be viewed by selecting your title from http://www.packtpub.com/support.

Piracy

Piracy of copyright material on the Internet is an ongoing problem across all media. At Packt, we take the protection of our copyright and licenses very seriously. If you come across any illegal copies of our works, in any form, on the Internet, please provide us with the location address or website name immediately so that we can pursue a remedy.

Please contact us at copyright@packtpub.com with a link to the suspected pirated material.

We appreciate your help in protecting our authors, and our ability to bring you valuable content.

Questions

You can contact us at questions@packtpub.com if you are having a problem with any aspect of the book, and we will do our best to address it.

Introduction to SciPy

There is no denying that the labor of scientists in the 21st century is so much easier than in previous generations. This is, among other reasons, because we have reinvented discovery into Networked Science; members of any scientific community with similar goals gather in large interdisciplinary teams and cooperate together to achieve complex mission-oriented goals. This new paradigm on the approach to research is also reflected in the computational resources employed by researchers. These are not restricted any more to a single piece of commercial software, created and maintained by a lone company, but libraries of code that sit on top of programming languages. The same professionals, who require fast and robust computational tools for their everyday work, get together and create these libraries in an open-source philosophy, in such a way that the resources are thoroughly tested, and improvements occur at faster pace than any commercial product could ever offer.

This book presents the most robust programming environment till date – a system based on two libraries of the computer language Python: NumPy and SciPy. In the following sections we wish to guide you on the usage of this system, through examples of state-of-the-art research in different branches of science and engineering.

What is SciPy?

The ideal programming environment for computational mathematics is one that enjoys the following characteristics:

- It must be based on a computer language that allows the user to work quickly, and integrate many systems effectively. Ideally, the underlying computer language should run on all different platforms (Windows, Mac OS X, Linux, Unix, iOS, Android, and so on.). This is key to fostering cooperation among scientists with different resources, as well as accessibility.

- It must contain a powerful set of libraries that allow the acquisition, storing, and handling of big datasets in a simple and effective way. This is key to allowing simulation and the employment of numerical computations at large scale.

- Smooth integration with other computer languages, as well as third-party software.

- Besides the usual running of compiled code, the programming environment should allow the possibility of interactive sessions, as well as scripting capabilities, for quick experimentation.

- Different coding paradigms should be supported; imperative, object-oriented, or functional coding styles should all be available to the user.

- It should be an open-source software; the user should be allowed to access the raw code of the libraries, and modify the basic algorithms if so desired. With commercial software, the inclusion of the improved algorithms is applied at the discretion of the seller, and it usually comes at a cost of the user. In the open-source universe, someone in the community usually performs these improvements, as they are published—at no cost.

- The set of applications should not be restricted to mere numerical computations; it should be powerful enough to allow symbolic computations as well.

Among the best-known environments for numerical computations used by the scientific community, we have the powerful MATLAB® and Scilab® systems (although both of them are commercial, expensive, and do not allow any tampering with the code). Maple® and Mathematica® are more geared towards symbolic computation, although they can match many of the numerical computations from MATLAB®. As the previous two, these are also commercial, expensive, and closed to modifications. A decent alternative to MATLAB®, based on similar mathematical engine, is the GNU Octave system. Most of the MATLAB® code is easily portable in Octave. It also has the advantage of being open source. Unfortunately, the underlying programming environment is not very user friendly. It is also restricted to numerical computations.

The one environment that combines the best of all worlds is indeed the combination of Python with the NumPy and SciPy libraries. The first property that attracts the user to Python is, without a doubt, its code readability. The syntax is extremely clear and expressive. It has the advantage of supporting code written in different paradigms – object oriented, functional, or old school imperative. It allows the compilation of code for running standalone executable programs, but it can also be used interactively, or as a scripting language. This is a great advantage if the user needs to develop tools for symbolic computation. Python has been used in this sense as the basis of a firm competitor to Maple® and Mathematica®: the open-source mathematics software **Sage (System for Algebra and Geometry Experimentation)**.

NumPy is an open-source extension to Python that adds support for multidimensional arrays of large sizes. This support allows the desired acquisition, storage, and complex manipulation of data mentioned previously. NumPy alone is a great tool to solve many numerical computations.

On top of NumPy, we have yet another open-source library, SciPy. This library contains algorithms and mathematical tools to manipulate NumPy objects, with very definite scientific and engineering objectives.

The combination of Python, NumPy, and SciPy (which henceforth should be coined "SciPy" for brevity) has been the environment of choice of many applied mathematicians for years; we work on a daily basis with both the pure mathematicians and with the hard-core engineers. One of the challenges of this trade is to bring to a single workstation the scientific production of professionals with different visions, techniques, tools, and software. SciPy is the perfect solution for coordinating everything together in a smooth, reliable, and coherent way.

Any day of the week, we are required to produce scripts in which, for example, there are combinations of experiments written and performed in SciPy itself, C/C++, Fortran, or MATLAB®. We often receive extremely large amounts of data from some signal acquisition devices. From all this heterogeneous material, we employ Python to retrieve the data, manipulate and, once finished with the analysis, produce high-quality documentation with professional-looking diagrams and visualization aids. SciPy allows performing all these tasks with ease.

This is partly because many dedicated software tools easily extend the core features of SciPy. For example, although any graphing and plotting is usually done with the Python libraries of matplotlib, there are also other packages, such as Biggles (`biggles. sourceforge.net`), Chaco (`pypi.python.org/pypi/chaco`), HippoDraw (`github. com/plasmodic/hippodraw`), MayaVi for 3D rendering (`mayavi.sourceforge.net`), or the **Python Imaging Library** or **PIL** (`pythonware.com/products/pil`).

Interfacing with non-Python packages is also possible. For example, the interaction of SciPy with the R statistical package can be done with RPy (`rpy.sourceforge. net/rpy2.html`). This allows for much more robust data analysis.

How to install SciPy

At the time when this book was written, the latest versions of Python are 2.7.3 and 3.2.3. They are both stable production releases, although the Python 2 versions are more convenient if the user needs to communicate with third-party applications. No new releases are done for Python 2, and that is why Python 3 is considered "the present and the future of Python". For the purposes of SciPy applications, we do recommend to stay with the 2.7.3 version. The language can be downloaded from the official Python site (`www.python.org/download`) and installed on all major systems such as Windows, Mac OS X, Linux, and Unix. It has also been ported to other platforms, including Palm OS, iOS, PlayStation, PSP, Psion, and so on. The following screenshot shows two popular options for coding in Python on an iPad – PythonMath and Sage Math. While the first application allows only the use of simple math libraries, the second permits the user to load and use both NumPy and SciPy remotely.

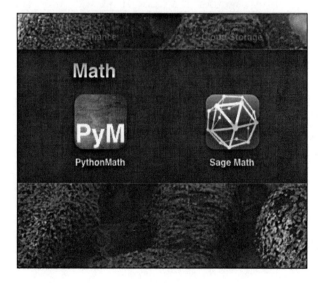

PythonMath and Sage Math bring Python coding to iOS devices. Sage Math allows importing NumPy and SciPy.

We shall not go into detail about the installation of Python on your system, since we already assume familiarity with this language. In case of doubt, we advise browsing the excellent book *Expert Python Programming: Best practices for designing, coding, and distributing your Python software, Tarek Ziadé, Packt Publishing*, where detailed explanations are given for installing any of the different implementations on different systems. It is usually a good idea to follow the directions given on the official Python website, as well. We will also assume familiarity with carrying out interactive sessions in Python, as well as writing standalone scripts.

The latest libraries for both NumPy and SciPy can be downloaded from the official SciPy site, `scipy.org/Download`. They both require a Python Version 2.4 or newer, so we should be in good shape at this point. We may choose to do the download from sourceforge (`sourceforge.net/projects/scipy`), or from Git repositories (for instance, the superpack from `fonnesbeck.github.com/ScipySuperpack`). It is also possible in some systems to use pre-packaged executable bundles that simplify the process. We will show here how to download and install in the most common cases.

For instance, in Mac OS X, if `macports` is installed, the process could not be easier. Open a terminal as superuser and, at the prompt (`%`), issue the following command:

```
% port search scipy
```

This presents a list of all ports that either install SciPy or use SciPy as a requirement. On that list, the one we require for Python 2.7 is the `py27-scipy` port. We install it (again as a superuser) by issuing the following command at prompt:

```
% port install py27-scipy
```

A few minutes later, the libraries are properly installed and ready to use. Note how `macports` also installs all needed requirements for us (including the NumPy libraries) without any extra effort from our part.

Under any other Unix/Linux system, if either no ports are available or if the user prefers to install from the packages downloaded from either sourceforge or Git, it is enough to perform the following steps:

1. Unzip the NumPy and SciPy packages following the recommendation of the official pages. This creates two folders, one for each library.

2. Within a terminal session, change directories to the folder where the NumPy libraries are stored, that contains the `setup.py` file. Find out which Fortran compiler you are using (one of `gnu`, `gnu95`, or `fcompiler`), and at prompt, issue the following command:

```
% python setup.py build -fcompiler=<compiler>
```

3. Once built, and on the same folder, issue the installation command. This should be all.

```
% python setup.py install
```

Under Microsoft Windows, we recommend you install from the binary installers provided by the Enthought Python Distribution. Download and double-click!

The procedure for the installation of the SciPy libraries is exactly the same, that is, downloading and building before installing under Unix/Linux, or downloading and double-clicking under Microsoft Windows. Note that different implementations of Python might have different requirements before installing NumPy and SciPy.

SciPy organization

SciPy is organized as a family of modules. We like to think of each module as a different field of mathematics. And as such, each has its own particular techniques and tools. The following is an exhaustive list of the different modules in SciPy:

scipy.constants	scipy.cluster	scipy.fftpack	scipy.integrate
scipy.interpolate	scipy.io	scipy.lib	scipy.linalg
scipy.misc	scipy.optimize	scipy.signal	scipy.sparse
scipy.spatial	scipy.special	scipy.stats	scipy.weave

The names of the modules are mostly self explanatory. For instance, the field of statistics deals with the study of the collection, organization, analysis, interpretation, and presentation of data. The objects with which statisticians deal for their research are usually represented as arrays of multiple dimensions. The result of certain operations on these arrays then offers information about the objects they represent (for example, the mean and standard deviation of a dataset). A well-known set of applications is based upon these operations; confidence intervals for the mean, hypothesis testing, or data mining, for instance. When facing any research problem that needs any tool of this branch of mathematics, we access the corresponding functions from the `scipy.stats` module.

Let us use some of its functions to solve a simple problem.

The following table shows the IQ test scores of 31 individuals:

114	100	104	89	102	91	114	114
103	105	108	130	120	132	111	128
118	119	86	72	111	103	74	112
107	103	98	96	112	112	93	

A stem plot of the distribution of these 31 scores shows that there are no major departures from normality, and thus we assume the distribution of the scores to be close to normal. Estimate the mean IQ score for this population, using a 99 percent confidence interval.

We start by loading the data into memory, as follows:

```
>>> scores=numpy.array([114, 100, 104, 89, 102, 91, 114, 114, 103, 105,
108, 130, 120, 132, 111, 128, 118, 119, 86, 72, 111, 103, 74, 112, 107,
103, 98, 96, 112, 112, 93])
```

At this point, if we type scores followed by a dot [.], and press the *Tab* key, the system offers us all possible methods inherited by the data from the NumPy library, as it is customary in Python. Technically, we could compute at this point the required mean, xmean, and corresponding confidence interval according to the formula, xmean $\pm$ zcrit * sigma / sqrt(n), where sigma and n are respectively the standard deviation and size of the data, and zcrit is the critical value corresponding to the confidence. In this case, we could look up a table on any statistics book to obtain a crude approximation to its value, zcrit = 2.576. The remaining values may be computed in our session and properly combined, as follows:

```
>>>xmean = numpy.mean(scores)
>>> sigma = numpy.std(scores)
>>> n = numpy.size(scores)
>>>xmean, xmean - 2.576*sigma /numpy.sqrt(n), \
... xmean + 2.756*sigma / numpy.sqrt(n)
(105.83870967741936, 99.343223715529746, 112.78807276397517)
```

We have thus computed the estimated mean IQ score (with value 105.83870967741936) and the interval of confidence (from about 99.34 to approximately 112.79). We have done so using purely NumPy-based operations, while following a known formula. But instead of making all these computations by hand, and looking for critical values on tables, we could directly ask SciPy for assistance.

Note how the `scipy.stats` module needs to be loaded before we use any of its functions, or request any help on them:

```
>>> from scipy import stats
>>> result=scipy.stats.bayes_mvs(scores)
```

The variable result contains the solution of our problem, and some more information. Note first that result is a tuple with three entries, as the help documentation suggests the following:

```
>>> help(scipy.stats.bayes_mvs)
```

This gives us the following output:

```
Help on function bayes_mvs in module scipy.stats.morestats:

bayes_mvs(data, alpha=0.90000000000000002)
    Return Bayesian confidence intervals for the mean, var, and std.

    Assumes 1-d data all has same mean and variance and uses Jeffrey's prior
    for variance and std.

    alpha gives the probability that the returned confidence interval contains
    the true parameter.

    Uses mean of conditional pdf as center estimate
    (but centers confidence interval on the median)

    Returns (center, (a, b)) for each of mean, variance and standard deviation.
    Requires 2 or more data-points.
(END)
```

The solution to our problem is then the first entry of the tuple `result`. To show the contents of this entry, we request it as usual:

```
>>> result[0]
(105.83870967741936, (98.789863768428674, 112.88755558641004))
```

Note how this output gives us the same average, but a slightly different confidence interval. This is, of course, more accurate than the one we computed in the previous steps.

How to find documentation

There is a wealth of information online, either from the official pages of SciPy (although its reference guides are somehow incomplete, as it is still a work in progress), or from many other contributors that present tutorials in forums, personal pages. There are other sources; many authors publish examples of their work with great detail online.

It is also possible to obtain help from within an interactive Python session, as we saw in the previous example. The code for the algorithms of the NumPy and SciPy libraries are written with docstrings, and this makes trivial requesting help for usage and recommendations, with the usual Python help system. For example, if in doubt of the usage of the bayes_mvs routine, the user can issue the following command at the command line:

```
>>>help(scipy.stats.bayes_mvs)
```

After executing this command, the system provides with the necessary information. Equivalently, both NumPy and SciPy come bundled with their own help system, info. For instance, look at the following command:

```
>>>numpy.info('random')
```

This will offer on screen a summary of all information parsed from the contents of all docstrings from the NumPy library associated with the given keyword (note it must be quoted). The user may navigate the output scrolling up and down, without possibility of further interaction.

This is convenient, provided we do already know the function we want to use, if we are unsure of its usage. But, what should we do if we don't know about the existence of this procedure, and suspect that it may exist? The usual Python way is to invoke the dir() command on a module, which offers a list of strings containing all possible names within. Interactive Python sessions make it easier to search for such information, with the possibility of navigating and performing further searches inside the output of help sessions. For instance, type in the following command at prompt:

```
>>>help(scipy.stats)
```

The results are shown as follows:

```
Help on package scipy.stats in scipy:

NAME
    scipy.stats

FILE
    /Applications/sage/local/lib/python2.6/site-packages/scipy/stats/__init__.py

DESCRIPTION
    Statistical Functions
    ======================

    This module contains a large number of probability distributions as
    well as a growing library of statistical functions.

    Each included distribution is an instance of the class rv_continous.
    For each given name the following methods are available.  See docstring for
    rv_continuous for more information

    :rvs:
        random variates with the distribution
    :pdf:
        probability density function
    :cdf:
        cumulative distribution function
    :sf:
        survival function (1.0 - cdf)
    :ppf:
        percent-point function (inverse of cdf)
    :isf:
        inverse survival function
    :stats:
        mean, variance, and optionally skew and kurtosis

    Calling the instance as a function returns a frozen pdf whose shape,
    location, and scale parameters are fixed.

    Distributions
    -------------

    The distributions available with the above methods are:
:
```

Note the colon (:) at the end of the screen—this is an old-school prompt. The system is in stand-by mode, expecting the user to issue a command (in the form of a single key). This also indicates that there are a few more pages of help following the given text. If we intend to read the rest of the help file, we may press Space bar to visit the next page. In this way we can visit the following manual pages on this topic. It is also possible to navigate the manual pages scrolling one line of text at a time, by using the up and down arrow keys. When we are ready to quit the help session, we simply press *Q*.

It is also possible to search the help contents for a given string. In that case, at the prompt, we press the (/) slash key. The prompt changes from a colon into a slash, and we proceed to input the keyword we would like to search for.

For example, is there a SciPy function that computes the Pearson kurtosis of a given dataset? At the slash prompt, we type in kurtosis and press enter. The help system takes us to the first occurrence of that string. To access successive occurrences of the string kurtosis, we press the *N* key (for next) until we find what we require. At that stage, we proceed to quit this help session (by pressing *Q*), and request more information on the function itself.

```
>>> help(scipy.stats.kurtosis)
```

The result is shown in the following screenshot:

```
Help on function kurtosis in module scipy.stats.stats:

kurtosis(a, axis=0, fisher=True, bias=True)
    Computes the kurtosis (Fisher or Pearson) of a dataset.

    Kurtosis is the fourth central moment divided by the square of the
    variance. If Fisher's definition is used, then 3.0 is subtracted from
    the result to give 0.0 for a normal distribution.

    If bias is False then the kurtosis is calculated using k statistics to
    eliminate bias coming from biased moment estimators

    Use kurtosistest() to see if result is close enough to normal.

    Parameters
    ----------
    a : array
        data for which the kurtosis is calculated
    axis : int or None
        Axis along which the kurtosis is calculated
    fisher : bool
        If True, Fisher's definition is used (normal ==> 0.0). If False,
        Pearson's definition is used (normal ==> 3.0).
    bias : bool
        If False, then the calculations are corrected for statistical bias.

    Returns
    -------
    kurtosis : array
        The kurtosis of values along an axis. If all values are equal,
        return -3 for Fisher's definition and 0 for Pearson's definition.


    References
    ----------
    [CRCProbStat2000]_ Section  2.2.25

    .. [CRCProbStat2000] Zwillinger, D. and Kokoska, S. (2000). CRC Standard
        Probablity and Statistics Tables and Formulae. Chapman & Hall: New
        York. 2000.
(END)
```

Scientific visualization

At this point we would like to introduce you to another resource, which we will be using to generate graphs for the examples – the matplotlib libraries. It may be downloaded from its official web page, matplotlib.org, and installed following the usual Python motions. There is a good online documentation in the official web page, and we encourage the reader to dig deeper than the few commands that we will use in this book. For instance, the excellent monograph *Matplotlib for Python Developers, Sandro Tosi, Packt Publishing*, provides all we shall need and more. Other plotting libraries are available (commercial or otherwise), which aim to very different and specific applications. The degree of sophistication and ease of use of matplotlib makes it one of the best options for generation of graphics in scientific computing.

Once installed, it may be imported as usual, with import matplotlib. Among all its modules, we will focus on pyplot, which provides a comfortable interface with the plotting libraries. For example, if we desire to plot at this point a cycle of the sine function, we could execute the following code snippet:

```
import numpy
import matplotlib.pyplot
x=numpy.linspace(0,numpy.pi,32)
fig=matplotlib.pyplot.figure()
fig.plot(x, numpy.sin(x))
fig.savefig('sine.png')
```

We obtain the following plot:

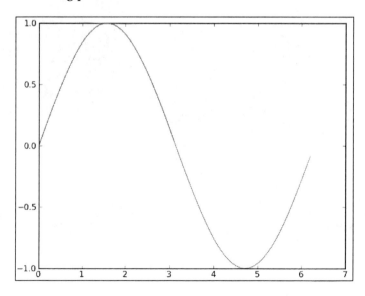

Let us explain each command from the previous session. The first two commands are used to import `numpy` and `matplotlib.pyplot` as usual. We define an array x of 32 uniformly spaced floating point values from 0 to π, and define y to be the array containing the sine of the values from x. The command figure creates space in memory to store the subsequent plots, and puts in place an object of the form `matplotlib.figure.Figure`. The command `plot(x, numpy.sin(x))` creates an object of the form `matplotlib.lines.Line2D`, containing data with the plot of x against `numpy.sin(x)`, together with a set of axes attached to it, labeled according to the ranges of the variables. This object is stored in the previous `Figure` object. The last command in the session, `savefig`, saves the `Figure` object to whatever valid image format we desire (in this case, a **Portable Network Graphics [PNG]** image). If instead of saving to a file we desire to show on screen the result of the plot, we issue the `fig.show()` command. From now on, in any code that deals with `matplotlib` commands, we will leave the option of showing/saving open.

There are, of course, commands that control the style of axes, aspect ratio between axes, labeling, colors, the possibility of managing several figures at the same time (subplots), and many more options to display all sort of data. We will be discovering these as we progress with examples through the book.

Summary

In this chapter we have learned the benefits of using the combination of Python, NumPy, SciPy, and matplotlib as a programming environment for any scientific endeavor that requires mathematics; in particular, anything related to numerical computations. We have explored the environment, learned how to download and install the required libraries, used them for some quick computations, and figured out a few good ways to search for help.

In the next chapter we will guide you through basic object creation in SciPy, including the best methods to manipulate data, or obtain information from it.

2
Top-level SciPy

At the top level, SciPy is basically NumPy, since both the object creation and basic manipulation of these objects are performed by functions of the latter library. This assures much faster computations, since the memory handling is done internally in an optimal way. For instance, if an operation must be made on the elements of a big multidimensional array, a novice user might be tempted to go over columns and rows with as many `for` loops as necessary. Loops run much faster when they access each consecutive element in the same order in which they are stored in memory. We should not be bothered with considerations of this kind when coding. The NumPy/SciPy operations assure that this is the case. As an added advantage, the names of operations in NumPy/SciPy are intuitive and self explanatory. Code written in this fashion is extremely easy to understand and maintain; faster to correct or change in case of need. Let us illustrate this point with one introductory example.

The `scipy.misc` library contains a classical image used in the image processing community for testing and comparison purposes – `scipy.misc.lena`. This is the name given to a 512 x 512 pixel standard test image, which has been in use since 1973, and was originally cropped from the centerfold of November 1972 issue of Playboy magazine. It is a picture of Lena Söderberg, a Swedish model, shot by photographer Dwight Hooker. The image is probably the most widely used test image for all sorts of image processing algorithms (such as compression and noise reduction) and related scientific publications.

This image is stored as a two-dimensional array. The nth column and m^{th} row entry of this array is a number that measures the grayscale value at the pixel in position ($n+1$, $m+1$) of the image. We access these numerical contents and store them in the `img` variable, by issuing the following command:

```
>>>img=scipy.misc.lena()
```

We may peek on some of these values, say the 7 x 3 upper corner of the image (7 columns, 3 rows). Instead of issuing a couple of `for` loops, we *slice* the corresponding portion of the image. The `img[0:3,0:7]` command gives us the following:

```
array([[162, 162, 162, 161, 162, 157, 163],
       [162, 162, 162, 161, 162, 157, 163],
       [162, 162, 162, 161, 162, 157, 163]])
```

We can use the same strategy to populate arrays, or change some of their values. For instance, in the next session, we change all entries of the second row of the previous array, between rows 2 and 6, to hold zeros, as follows:

```
>>>img[1,1:6]=0
>>> print img[0:3,0:7]
[[162 162 162 161 162 157 163]
 [162   0   0   0   0   0 163]
 [162 162 162 161 162 157 163]]
```

Object essentials

We have been introduced to the basic object – the multidimensional array (which in NumPy jargon is referred to as `ndarray`). All elements of the array are casted to the same datatype. We obtain this datatype by issuing the `dtype` command. We are able to access the value of any of its elements, as well as its dimension (shape), size, and many other properties of the array. The following session illustrates how to obtain some of that information:

```
>>>img.dtype, img.shape, img.size
```

```
(dtype('int64'), (512, 512), 262144)
>>>img[32,67]
87
```

Let us interpret the outputs. The entries of img are 64-bit integer values ('int64'). This is essentially different on different systems, and depends on both the Python installation and our computer specifications. The shape of the array (note it comes as a Python tuple) is 512 x 512, and consequently it has 262144 entries. The grayscale value of the image at the 33rd column and 68th row is 87 (note that in NumPy, as in Python or C, all indices are zero based).

We will now introduce the basic property and methods of NumPy/SciPy objects – datatype and indexing.

Datatype

There are several formulae to impose the datatype. For instance, if we want all entries of an already-created array to be 32-bit floating point values, we may cast it as follows:

```
>>> img=scipy.misc.lena().astype('float32')
```

A second way is done by using the optional argument, dtype= on any array creation command:

```
>>> scores = numpy.array([101,103,84], dtype='float32')
```

This can be simplified even further with a third clever method (although this practice offers codes that are not so easy to interpret):

```
>>> scores = numpy.float32([101,103,84])
array([ 101.,   103.,    84.], dtype=float32)
```

The choice of datatypes for NumPy arrays is extremely flexible; we may choose the basic Python types (including bool, dict, list, set, tuple, str, and unicode), although for numerical computations we mainly focus on int, float, long, and complex.

NumPy has its own datatypes optimized for using them with ndarray instances, with the same precision as the previously given native types. We distinguish them with a trailing underscore (_) after the name. For instance, ndarray of strings could be initialized, as follows:

```
>>> a=numpy.array(['Cleese', 'Idle', 'Gilliam'], dtype='str_')
>>>a.dtype
dtype('|S7')
```

Note two things; unlike its purely Python counterpart, the usage of the `'str_'` datatype requires the name to be quoted. We could use the longer unquoted version, `numpy.str_`, instead. Also, when prompted for datatype, the system returns its C-derived equivalent name instead; `'|S7'` (`'|S` for strings, and `7'` to indicate the largest size of any of its elements).

The most common way to address the usual numerical types is with the bit width nomenclature – `boolXX`, `intXX`, `uintXX`, `floatXX`, or `complexXX`, where `XX` indicates the bit size (for example, `uint32` for 32-bit unsigned integers).

It is also possible to design our own datatypes, and this is where the full potential of the flexibility of NumPy datatypes arise. For instance, a datatype to indicate the name and grades of a student could be created, as follows:

```
>>> dt=numpy.dtype([ ('name', numpy.str_, 16), 'grades', numpy.float64,
(2,)) ])
```

This means that the `dt` datatype has two parts – the first part is a name, that must be a 16 characters, `numpy.str_` string. The second part, the grades, is a subarray of dimension 2 with scores as 64-bit floating point values. A valid array with elements in this datatype would then look like the following:

```
>>> MA141 = numpy.array([ ('Cleese', (7.0,8.0)), ('Gilliam', (9.0,10.0))
], dtype=dt)
```

Indexing

There are two basic methods to access the data in a NumPy array `A`, both of them with the same syntax, `A[obj]`, where `obj` is a Python object that performs the selection. We are already familiar with the basic method of record access for a single entry. The second method is the objective of this subsection, slicing. This concept is what makes NumPy and SciPy so incredibly easy to manage.

The basic slice is a Python object of the form `slice(start,stop,step)`, or in a more compact notation, `start:stop:step`. Initially, the three variables `start`, `stop`, and `step` are non-negative integer values, with `start` less than or equal to `stop`. This represents the sequence of indices *start + (k * step)*, for indices `k` from 0 to the largest integer smaller or equal to the value given by *(stop - start) / step*. When a slice is placed on any of the dimensions of `ndarray`, it selects all entries in that dimension indexed by the corresponding sequence of indices. The simple examples given next illustrate this point:

```
>>> A=numpy.array([[1,2,3,4,5,6,7,8],[2,4,6,8,10,12,14,16]])
>>> print A[0:2, 0:8:2]
```

```
[[ 1   3   5   7]
 [ 2   6  10  14]]
```

If `start` is greater than `stop`, a negative value of `step` is used to traverse the sequence backwards.

```
>>> print A[0:2, 8:0:-2]
[[ 8,   6,   4,   2]
 [16,  12,   8,   4]]
```

Negative values of `start` and `stop` are interpreted as `n-start` and `n-stop` (respectively), where n is the size of the corresponding dimension. The `A[0:2,-1:0:-2]` command gives exactly the same output as the previous example.

The slice objects can be shortened by absence of start (which implies a zero if `step` is positive, or the size of the dimension if `step` is negative), absence of `stop` (which implies the size of the corresponding dimension in case of positive `step`, or zero in case of negative `step`). Absence of `step` implies `step` is equal to 1. The `::` object can be shortened simply as `:`, for an easier syntax. The `A[:, ::-2]` command then offers yet again the same output as the previous two.

The first nonbasic method of accessing data from an array is based on the idea of collecting several indices, and requesting the elements in array with those indices. For example, from our previous array A we would like to construct a new array with the elements on locations (0, 0), (0, 3), (1, 2), and (1, 5). We do so by gathering the x and y values of the indices in respective lists – `[0,0,1,1]`, `[0,3,2,5]`, and feeding these lists to A as an indexing object, as follows:

```
>>> print A[ [0,0,1,1], [0,3,2,5] ]
[ 1   4   6  12]
```

Note how the result loses the dimension of the primitive array, and offers a one-dimensional array. If we desire to capture a subarray of A with indices in the Cartesian product of two sets of indices, respecting the row and column choice and creating a new array with the dimensions of the Cartesian product, we use the comfortable `ix_` command. For instance, if in our previous array we would like to obtain the subarray of dimension 2 x 2 with indices in the Cartesian product of indices (0, 1) by (0,3) (these are the locations (0, 0), (0, 3), (1, 0), and (1, 3)), we do so as follows:

```
>>> print A[ numpy.ix_( [0,1], [0,3] )]
[[1 4]
 [2 8]]
```

The array object

At this point we are ready for a thorough study of all interesting attributes of `ndarray` for Scientific computing purposes. We have already covered a few, such as `dtype`, `shape`, and `size`. Other useful attributes are `ndim` (to compute the number of dimensions in the array), `real` and `imag` (to obtain the real and imaginary parts of the data, should this be formed by complex numbers), or `flat` (which creates a one-dimensional indexable iterator from the data).

For instance, if we desired to add all the values of an array together, we could use the `flat` attribute to run over all the elements sequentially, and accumulate all the values in a variable. A possible code to perform this task should look like the following code snippet (compare this code with the `ndarray.sum()` method explained in object calculation ahead):

```
>>> value=0; img=scipy.misc.lena()
>>> for item in img.flat: value+=item
>>> value
32518120
```

We have also explored some of the methods applied to arrays. These are the tools used to modify these objects; let it be their datatypes, their shape, or converting them to a different structure. We classify these methods in three big categories – array conversion, shape selection/manipulation, and object calculation.

Array conversion is used to cast data to different types (`astype`), copy arrays to store them under another variables (`copy`), fill whole arrays with scalar values (`fill`), or dump the array to a file, list, or string (`tofile`, `tolist`, `tostring`).

For instance, to write the contents of the `img` array to a text file, making sure that each entry of the array is printed as an integer, and that every two integers are separated by a white space, we could issue the following command:

```
>>> img.tofile("lena.txt",sep=" ",format="%i")
```

Note how the formatting string follows C conventions.

Shape selection/manipulation is usually employed when we require some kind of rearranging (`swapaxes`, `transpose`), including sorting (`argsort`, `sort`). We also use these methods when we need reshaping (`reshape`), resizing (`flatten`, `ravel`, `resize`, `squeeze`) or selecting (`choose`, `compress`, `diagonal`, `nonzero`, `searchsorted`, `take`). These methods are very powerful when used in cooperation with slicing operations; as a matter of fact, many of them can be used instead of slicing to offer our users more readable code.

We need to say a word about the differences between `flat`, `ravel`, and `flatten`, which offer very similar outputs, since they make a huge difference of usage in terms of memory management. The first one, `flat`, creates an iterator to the elements of the array. Once used, it disappears from memory. The second one, `ravel`, returns a view of the one-dimensional flattened array when it can, and copies of it when requested. The last one, `flatten`, creates a copy of the flattened one-dimensional array, and always allocates memory for it. We use it only when we need to change the values of flattened arrays.

Notice also the power of the sorting methods in the session given next. We create an array of integers. If these values were sorted, what would be the order of their indices? We may obtain this information with the `argsort` method. We may even impose the sorting algorithm to be used (rather than coding it ourselves) – `quicksort`, `mergesort`, or `heapsort`. We can even sort the array in place, using the `sort` method, as follows:

```
>>> A=numpy.array([11,13,15,17,19,18,16,14,12,10])
>>>A.argsort(kind='mergesort')
array([9, 0, 8, 1, 7, 2, 6, 3, 5, 4])
>>>A.sort()
>>> print A
[10 11 12 13 14 15 16 17 18 19]
```

Array calculation methods are used to perform computations or extract information about our data. We have a set of methods of statistical nature that help us compute, for instance, maximum or minimum values of the data (`max`, `min`), as well as their corresponding indices (`argmax`, `argmin`). We have methods to compute the sum, cumulative sums, product, or cumulative products (`sum`, `cumsum`, `prod`, `cumprod`). It is possible to extract the average (`mean`), point spread (`ptp`), variance (`var`), or standard deviation (`std`). Further nonstatistical calculation methods allow us to compute complex conjugate of complex-valued arrays (`conj`), the trace of the array (`trace`, the sum of the elements in the diagonal), or even clipping the matrix (`clip`) by forcing a minimum and maximum value below and above certain thresholds.

Note how most of these methods can act on the whole array, or over each of its dimensions:

```
>>> A=numpy.array([[1,1,1],[2,2,2],[3,3,3]])
>>>A.mean()
2
>>>A.mean(axis=0)
array([ 2.,   2.,   2.])
>>>A.mean(axis=1)
array([ 1.,   2.,   3.])
```

Let us also illustrate the `clip` command with an easy exercise based on the Lena image.

Compute the maximum and minimum values of Lena (`img`), and contrast them with the point spread (it should be equal to the difference between those two values). Create a new array A by clipping Lena so that the minimum is maintained, but the point spread is reduced to only 100 values.

```
>>>img.min(), img.max(), img.ptp()
(25, 245, 220)
>>> A=img.clip(img.min(),img.min()+100)
>>>A.min(), A.max(), A.ptp()
(25, 125, 100)
```

Array routines

In this section we will deal with most operations with arrays. We will classify them in four main categories, as follows:

- Routines for the creation of new arrays
- Routines for the manipulation of a single array
- Routines for the combination of two or more arrays
- Routines to extract information from arrays

The reader will surely realize that some operations of this kind can be carried out by methods, which once again shows the flexibility of Python and NumPy.

Routines for array creation

We have seen the basic command that brings an array to memory and stores it to a variable – `A=numpy.array([[1,2],[2,1]])`. The complete syntax is as follows:

```
array(object=,dtype=None,copy=True,order=None,subox=False,ndim=0)
```

Let us go over the options; `object` is simply the data we use to initialize the array. In the previous example, that object is a small 2 x 2 square matrix; we may impose a determinate datatype with the `dtype` option. The result is stored in the variable A; if `copy` is false, the returned object will be a copy of the array only if `dtype` is not equivalent to the datatype of `object`. The arrays are stored following a C-style ordering of rows and columns. If the user prefers to store the array following the memory style of Fortran, the `order='Fortran'` option should be used. The `subok` option is very subtle; if true, the array may be passed as a subclass of the object.

If false, then only `ndarray` arrays are passed. And finally, the `ndim` option indicates the smallest dimension returned by the array. If not offered, this is computed from `object`.

A set of special arrays can be obtained with the commands such as `zeros`, `ones`, `identity`, and `eye`. The names of these commands are quite informative, as mentioned next:

- `zeros` creates an array filled with zeros
- `ones` creates an array filled with ones
- The `identity` command creates a square matrix with dimension indicated by a single positive integer n. The entries are filled with zeros, except along the main diagonal ((k, k) for k from 0 to n-1), which is filled with ones.
- Very similar to `identity` is the `eye` command, which also constructs diagonal arrays. Unlike `identity`, `eye` allows specifying diagonals off the main one, and nonsquare arrays.

```
>>> Z=numpy.zeros((5,5), dtype=int)
>>> U=numpy.ones((2,2), dtype=int)
>>> I=numpy.identity(3, dtype=int)
```

In the first two cases, we indicated the shape of the array (as a Python tuple of positive integers), and the optional datatype imposition.

The syntax for `eye` is as follows:

```
numpy.eye(N,M=None,k=0,dtype=float)
```

The integers, `N` and `M` indicate the shape of the array, and the integer `k` indicates the index of the diagonal to populate. An index `k=0` (the default) points to the main diagonal, a positive index refers to upper diagonals, and negative value refer to lower diagonals.

```
>>> D=numpy.eye(4,k=1) + numpy.eye(4,k=-1)
>>> print D
[[ 0.  1.  0.  0.]
 [ 1.  0.  1.  0.]
 [ 0.  1.  0.  1.]
 [ 0.  0.  1.  0.]]
```

With the aid of only the previous four commands and basic slicing, it is possible to create more complex arrays in simple ways. We propose the following challenge.

Use exclusively the previous definitions of U and I, together with an eye array. How would the reader create a 5 x 5 array A of floating values with "fives" at the four entries (0, 0), (0, 1), (1, 0), (1, 1); "sixes" along the remaining entries of the diagonal; and "threes" in the two other corners?

```
>>> A=3.0*(numpy.eye(5,k=4) + numpy.eye(5,k=-4))
>>> A[0:2,0:2]=5*U; A[2:5,2:5]=6*I
>>> print A
[[ 5.  5.  0.  0.  3.]
 [ 5.  5.  0.  0.  0.]
 [ 0.  0.  6.  0.  0.]
 [ 0.  0.  0.  6.  0.]
 [ 3.  0.  0.  0.  6.]]
```

The flexibility of array creation in NumPy is even more apparent with the fromfunction command. For instance, if we require a 4 x 4 array where each entry reflects the product of its indices, we use the lambda function, (lambda i,j: i*j) in the fromfunction command, as follows:

```
>>> B=numpy.fromfunction( (lambda i,j: i*j), (4,4), dtype=int)
>>> print B
[[0 0 0 0]
 [0 1 2 3]
 [0 2 4 6]
 [0 3 6 9]]
```

Of great importance are the array creation commands that deal with the concept of masking. This is one of the most reliable methods to manipulate large arrays of data, and it is based on the idea of gathering those indices for which their corresponding entries satisfy a given condition. For example, in the array B shown in the preceding code snippet, we can mask all zero-valued entries with the B==0 command, as follows:

```
>>> print B==0
[[ True  True  True  True]
 [ True False False False]
 [ True False False False]
 [ True False False False]]
```

How would the reader update B so that those zero entries can be replaced by the sum of the squares of their corresponding indices?

Multiplying a mask by a second array of the same shape offers a new array in which each entry is either zero (if the corresponding entry in the mask is false) or the entry of the second array (if the corresponding entry in the mask is true).

```
>>> B += numpy.fromfunction((lambda i,j:i*i+j*j), (4,4))*(B==0)
>>> print B
[[0 1 4 9]
 [1 1 2 3]
 [4 2 4 6]
 [9 3 6 9]]
```

But note that, in this process, we have created in each step a new array in memory with as many Boolean values as the size of the original array. In these toy examples it is not a big deal. But when handling large datasets, allocating too much memory could seriously slow down our computations and exhaust the memory of our system. Among the creation commands presented in the table, there are two in particular, such as putmask and where, which facilitate the management of resources internally, thus speeding up the process.

Note, for example, when we look for all odd-valued entries in B, the resulting mask has size of 16, although the interesting entries are only eight.

```
>>> print B%2!=0
[[False  True False  True]
 [ True  True False  True]
 [False False False False]
 [ True  True False  True]]
```

The numpy.where() command helps us gather precisely those entries in a more efficient way.

```
>>>numpy.where(B%2!=0)
(array([0, 0, 1, 1, 1, 3, 3, 3]), array([1, 3, 0, 1, 3, 0, 1, 3]))
```

If we desire to change those odd entries to, say their squares plus one, we can use the numpy.putmask() command instead, for a better management of memory.

```
>>>numpy.putmask( B, B%2!=0, B^2+1)
>>> print B
[[ 0  2  4 82]
 [ 2  2  2 10]
 [ 4  2  4  6]
 [82 10  6 82]]
```

Note how the `putmask` procedure does update the values of B, without the explicit need to make an assignment.

There are three more interesting commands that create arrays in the form of meshes. The `arange` and `linspace` commands create uniformly spaced values between two numbers. In `arange` we specify the spacing between elements; in `linspace` we specify the desired number of elements in the mesh. The `logspace` command creates uniformly spaced values in a logarithmic scale between the logarithm of two numbers to the base 10. The user could think of these outputs as the support of univariate functions.

```
>>> L1=numpy.arange(-1,1,0.3)
>>> print L1
[-1.  -0.7 -0.4 -0.1  0.2  0.5  0.8]
>>>L2=numpy.linspace(-1,1,4)
>>> print L2
[-1.         -0.33333333  0.33333333  1.        ]
>>>L3= numpy.logspace(-1,1,4)
>>> print L3
[ 0.1         0.46415888  2.15443469 10.        ]
>>> L3
```

Finally, `meshgrid`, `mgrid`, and `ogrid` create two two-dimensional arrays of dimensions *n x m*, containing the elements of two given one-dimensional arrays of dimensions *n* and *m*. It accomplished this by repeating the values of each array as necessary. The user could think of these outputs as the support of functions of two variables.

The first of these routines, `meshgrid`, accepts only arrays as input. The other two routines, `mgrid` and `ogrid`, accept only indexing objects (for example, slices). The difference between these last two is a matter of memory allocation; while `mgrid` allocates full arrays with all the data, `ogrid` only creates enough sets so that the corresponding `mgrid` command could be obtained by a proper Cartesian product, as follows:

```
>>> print numpy.meshgrid(L2,L3)
(array([[-1.        , -0.33333333,  0.33333333,  1.        ],
        [-1.        , -0.33333333,  0.33333333,  1.        ],
        [-1.        , -0.33333333,  0.33333333,  1.        ],
        [-1.        , -0.33333333,  0.33333333,  1.        ]]), array([[
0.1       ,  0.1       ,  0.1       ,  0.1       ],
```

```
     [  0.46415888,     0.46415888,     0.46415888,     0.46415888],
     [  2.15443469,     2.15443469,     2.15443469,     2.15443469],
     [ 10.        ,  10.        ,  10.        ,  10.        ]]))
>>> print numpy.mgrid[0:5,0:5]
[[[0 0 0 0 0]
  [1 1 1 1 1]
  [2 2 2 2 2]
  [3 3 3 3 3]
  [4 4 4 4 4]]

 [[0 1 2 3 4]
  [0 1 2 3 4]
  [0 1 2 3 4]
  [0 1 2 3 4]
  [0 1 2 3 4]]]
>>> print numpy.ogrid[0:5,0:5]
[array([[0],
        [1],
        [2],
        [3],
        [4]]), array([[0, 1, 2, 3, 4]])]
```

We would like to finish the subsection on array creation by showing one of the most useful routines for image processing and differential equations – the tile command. Its syntax is very simple, and is shown as follows:

```
    tile(A, reps)
```

This routine presents a very effective way of tiling an array A following some repetition pattern reps (a tuple, a list, or another array) to create larger arrays. The following checkerboards exercise shows its potential.

Start with two small binary arrays – B=numpy.ones((3,3)) and checker2by2=numpy.zeros((6,6)), and create a checkerboard using tile and as few operations as possible.

The following is a possible solution:

```
>>>checker2by2[0:3,0:3]=checker2by2[3:6,3:6]=B
>>> numpy.tile(checker2by2,(4,4))
```

Routines for the combination of two or more arrays

On occasion we need to combine the data of two or more arrays together to solve a specific problem. The core NumPy libraries contain extremely efficient routines to carry out these computations, and we urge the reader to get familiar with them. They are constructed with state-of-the-art algorithms, and they make sure that usage of memory is minimum and complexity is optimal. The most relevant in this set of routines are those that operate on arrays as if they were matrices. We then have matrix products (outer, inner, dot, vdot, tensordot, cross, and kron), array correlations (correlate, convolve), array stacking (concatenate, vstack, hstack, column_stack, row_stack, and dstack), and array comparison (allclose).

The reader versed in linear algebra will surely enjoy the matrix products included in NumPy. We postpone their usage and analysis until we cover the SciPy module on linear algebra in *Chapter 3, SciPy for Linear Algebra*.

An excellent use for correlation of arrays is, for example, for basic pattern matching. For instance, the image in the following example represents a binary array (it contains only ones and zeros). We visualize it by assigning to each location in the array a white pixel if the corresponding value is one, and a black pixel to zero values. The first array, text, contains an image of a paragraph extracted from the wikipedia page on Don Quixote, while a second array, letterE, contains an image of the letter "e". This letterE array is actually a subarray of dimension 6 x 6 obtained from the text array:

```
>>>letterE=text[14:20,169:175]
```

The maximum value of the correlation of both arrays offers the location of all the "e" letters contained in the array text:

```
>>> print letterE
[[0 1 1 1 1 0]
 [1 0 0 0 0 1]
 [1 1 1 1 1 1]
 [1 0 0 0 0 0]
 [1 0 0 0 0 0]
 [0 1 1 1 1 1]]
>>>corr = scipy.ndimage.correlate(text,letterE)
>>> eLocations = (corr == corr.max())
```

This results in the following screenshot:

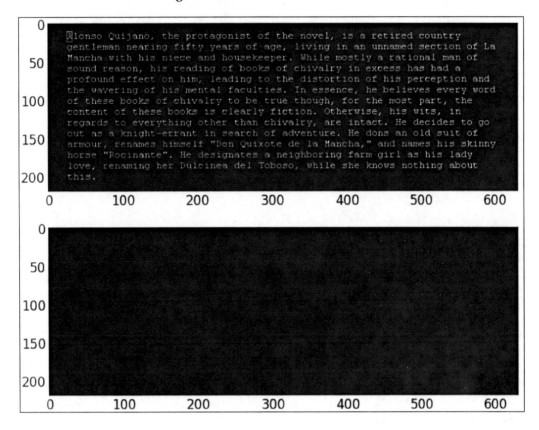

A few words about stacking operations; we have a basic concatenation routine, concatenate, which joins a sequence of arrays together along a pre-determined axis. Of course, all arrays in the sequence must have the same dimensions, otherwise it doesn't work. The rest of the stack operations are syntactic sugar for special cases of concatenate – vstack to glue arrays vertically, hstack to glue arrays horizontally, dstack to glue arrays in the third dimension, and so on.

Another impressive set of routines for array combination are the set operations. They allow the user to handle one-dimensional arrays as if they were sets, and perform with easiness, the Boolean operations of intersection (intersect1d), union (union1d), set difference (setdiff1d), or set exclusive or (setxor1d). The results of any of these set operations on arrays always return sorted arrays. It is also possible to test whether all the elements in one array belong to a second array (in1d).

Routines for array manipulation

There is a sequence of splitting routines, designed to break up arrays into smaller arrays, in any given dimension – `array_split`, `split` (both basic splitting in the indicated axis), `hsplit` (horizontal split), `vsplit` (vertical split), and `dsplit` (in the third axis). Let us illustrate these with a simple example:

```
>>> print checker2by2
[[ 1.  1.  1.  0.  0.  0.]
 [ 1.  1.  1.  0.  0.  0.]
 [ 1.  1.  1.  0.  0.  0.]
 [ 0.  0.  0.  1.  1.  1.]
 [ 0.  0.  0.  1.  1.  1.]
 [ 0.  0.  0.  1.  1.  1.]]
>>>numpy.vsplit(checker2by2,3)
[array([[ 1.,  1.,  1.,  0.,  0.,  0.],
        [ 1.,  1.,  1.,  0.,  0.,  0.]]),
 array([[ 1.,  1.,  1.,  0.,  0.,  0.],
        [ 0.,  0.,  0.,  1.,  1.,  1.]]),
 array([[ 0.,  0.,  0.,  1.,  1.,  1.],
        [ 0.,  0.,  0.,  1.,  1.,  1.]])]
```

The behavior of a Python function on an array is *usually* the application of the function to each of the elements of the array. Note for example how the NumPy function `sin` works on an array:

```
>>> a=numpy.array([-numpy.pi, numpy.pi])
>>> print numpy.vstack((a, numpy.sin(a)))
[[ -3.14159265e+00    3.14159265e+00]
 [ -1.22464680e-16    1.22464680e-16]]
```

This happens provided the function has been properly vectorized (which is the case with `numpy.sin`). Notice the behavior with nonvectorized Python functions. Let us define one that computes, for each value of x, the maximum between x and 100 without using any routine from the NumPy libraries.

```
# function max100
defmax100(x):
    return max(x,100)
```

If we try to apply this function to the preceding array, the system raises an error, as follows:

```
>>> max100(a)
ValueError: The truth value of an array with more than one element is
ambiguous. Use a.any() or a.all()
```

We need to explicitly indicate to the system when we desire to apply one of our functions to arrays, as well as scalars. We do that with the `vectorize` routine, as follows:

```
>>>numpy.vectorize(max100)(a)
array([100, 100])
```

For our benefit, the NumPy libraries provide a great deal of already-vectorized mathematical functions. Some examples are `round_`, `fix` (to round the elements of an array to a desired number of decimal places), `angle` (to provide the angle of the elements of an array, provided they are complex numbers), any basic trigonometric (`sin`, `cos`, `tan`, `sic`), exponential (`exp`, `exp2`, `sinh`, `cosh`), and logarithmic functions (`log`, `log10`, `log2`).

We also have mathematical functions that treat the array as output of multidimensional functions, and offer relevant computations. Some useful examples are `diff` (to emulate differentiation along any specified dimension, by performing discrete differences), `gradient` (to compute the gradient of the corresponding function), or `cov` (for the covariance of the array). Sorting the whole array according to the values of the first axis is also possible with the `msort` and `sort_complex` routines.

Routines to extract information from arrays

Most of the routines to extract information are statistical in nature, which include `average` (which acts exactly as the `mean` method), `median` (to compute the statistical median of the array on any of its dimensions, or the array as a whole), and computation of histograms (`histogram`, `histogram2d`, and `histogramdd`, depending on the dimensions of the array). The other important set of routines in this category deal with the concept of bins for arrays of dimension one. This is more easily explained by means of examples. Take the array `A=numpy.array([5,1,1,2,1,1,2,2,10,3,3,4,5])`. The `unique` command finds the different values in any array, and presents them as sorted:

```
>>>numpy.unique(A)
array([ 1, 2, 3, 4, 5, 10])
```

For arrays such as A, in which all the entries are nonnegative integers, we can visualize the array A as a sequence of eleven bins labeled with numbers from 0 to 10 (the maximum value in the array). Each bin with label *n* contains the number of *n*'s in the array:

```
>>>numpy.bincount(A)
array([0, 4, 3, 2, 1, 2, 0, 0, 0, 0, 1])
```

For arrays where some of the elements are not numbers (nan), NumPy has a set of routines that mimic methods to extract information, but disregard the conflicting elements – nanmax, nanmin, nanargmax, nanargmin, nansum, and so on.

```
>>> A=numpy.fromfunction((lambda i,j: (i+1)*(-1)**(i*j)), (4,4))
>>> print A
[[ 1.   1.   1.   1.]
 [ 2.  -2.   2.  -2.]
 [ 3.   3.   3.   3.]
 [ 4.  -4.   4.  -4.]]
>>> B=numpy.log2(A)
>>> print B
[[ 0.          0.          0.          0.        ]
 [ 1.                 nan  1.                nan]
 [ 1.5849625   1.5849625   1.5849625   1.5849625]
 [ 2.                 nan  2.                nan]]
>>>numpy.sum(B), numpy.nansum(B)
(nan, 12.339850002884624)
```

Summary

In this chapter we have explored in depth the creation and basic manipulation of the object array used by SciPy, as an overview of the NumPy libraries. In particular, we have seen the principles of slicing and masking, which simplify the coding of algorithms to the point of transforming an otherwise unreadable sequence of loops and primitive commands, into an intuitive and self-explanatory set of object calls and methods. We have also learned that the nonbasic modules in NumPy are replicated as modules in SciPy itself. The chapter roughly followed the same structure as the official NumPy reference (which the reader can access at the SciPy pages at `docs.scipy.org/doc/numpy/reference`). There are other good sources that cover NumPy with rigor, and we refer you to any of that other material for a more detailed coverage of this topic.

In the next five chapters we will be accessing the commands that make SciPy a powerful tool in numerical computing. The structure of those chapters is basically a reflection of the different SciPy modules, structured in an order that allows building applications on top of each other.

3
SciPy for Linear Algebra

In the following chapters, we will continue exploring the different SciPy modules through meaningful examples. We will start with the treatment of matrices (whether normal or sparse) with the modules on Linear Algebra – `linalg` and `sparse.linalg` – which expand and improve the NumPy module with the same name.

This discipline of mathematics mainly studies vector spaces and the linear mappings among them. Matrices represent objects in this field naturally, in such a way that any property of the underlying objects may be obtained by performing some operation on the representing matrices. We assume at this point that you are familiar with at least the basics of linear algebra, in particular with the notion of matrix multiplication, finding the determinant and inverse of a matrix, as well as their immediate applications in vector calculus.

Matrix creation

In SciPy, a matrix structure is given to any one- or two-dimensional `ndarray`, with either the `matrix` or `mat` command. The complete syntax is as follows:

```
numpy.matrix(data=object, dtype=None, copy=True)
```

In the creation of matrices, the data may be given as a string or as `ndarray`, which is very convenient. When using strings, the semicolon denotes change of row, and the comma denotes change of column:

```
>>> A=numpy.matrix("1,2,3;4,5,6")
>>> A
matrix([[1, 2, 3],
        [4, 5, 6]])
```

```
>>> A=numpy.matrix([[1,2,3],[4,5,6]])
>>> A
matrix([[1, 2, 3],
        [4, 5, 6]])
```

Another way of creating a matrix from a two-dimensional array is by enforcing the matrix structure on a new object, copying the data of the former with the asmatrix routine.

We say that a matrix is sparse if most of its entries are zeros. It is a waste of memory to input such matrices in the usual way, especially if the dimensions are large, and SciPy contemplates different procedures to store such matrices effectively in memory. Most of the usual methods to input sparse matrices are contemplated in SciPy as routines in the scipy.sparse module. Some of those methods are block sparse row (bsr_matrix), coordinate format (coo_matrix), compressed sparse column or row (csc_matrix, csr_matrix), sparse matrix with diagonal storage (dia_matrix), dictionary with keys-based sorting (dok_matrix), and row-based linked list (lil_matrix).

At this point, we would like to present at least one of them: the coordinate format. In this format, given a sparse matrix A, we identify the coordinates of the nonzero elements, say *n* of them, and we create two *n*-dimensional ndarray arrays containing in order, the columns and rows of those entries, and a third ndarray containing the values of the corresponding entries. For instance, notice the following sparse matrix:

$$
\begin{pmatrix}
0 & 10 & 0 & 0 & 0 \\
0 & 0 & 20 & 0 & 0 \\
0 & 0 & 0 & 30 & 0 \\
0 & 0 & 0 & 0 & 40 \\
0 & 0 & 0 & 0 & 0
\end{pmatrix}
$$

One of the nonzero entries is at the second column and first row (this is the location (1, 0) in Python) and has the value, 10. Another nonzero entry is at (2, 1) and has the value, 20. A third nonzero entry, with the value 30, is located at (3, 2). The last nonzero entry of A is located at (4, 3), and has the value, 40.

We then have ndarray of rows, another ndarray of columns, and another ndarray of values:

```
>>> rows=numpy.array([0,1,2,3])
>>> cols=numpy.array([1,2,3,4])
>>> vals=numpy.array([10,20,30,40])
```

We create the matrix A as follows:

```
>>> import scipy.sparse
>>> A=scipy.sparse.coo_matrix( (vals,(rows,cols)) )
>>> print A; print A.todense()
  (0, 1)    10.0
  (1, 2)    20.0
  (2, 3)    30.0
  (3, 4)    40.0
[[  0.  10.   0.   0.   0.]
 [  0.   0.  20.   0.   0.]
 [  0.   0.   0.  30.   0.]
 [  0.   0.   0.   0.  40.]]
```

Notice how the `todense` method turns sparse matrices into full matrices. Also note that it obviates any row or column of full zeros following the last nonzero element.

Associated to each input method, we have functions that identify sparse matrices of each kind. For instance, if we suspect that A is a sparse matrix in the `coo_matrix` format, we may use the following command:

```
>>> scipy.sparse.isspmatrix_coo(A)
True
```

All the array routines cast to matrices, provided the input is a matrix. This is very convenient for matrix creation, especially thanks to stacking commands (`hstack`, `vstack`, `tile`). Besides these, matrices enjoy one more amazing stacking command, `bmat`. This routine allows the stacking of matrices by means of strings, making use of the convention "semicolon for change of row, comma for change of column", and allowing matrix names inside of the string to be evaluated. The following example is enlightening:

```
>>> B=numpy.mat(numpy.ones((3,3)))
>>> W=numpy.mat(numpy.zeros((3,3)))
>>> print numpy.bmat('B,W;W,B')
[[ 1.  1.  1.  0.  0.  0.]
 [ 1.  1.  1.  0.  0.  0.]
 [ 1.  1.  1.  0.  0.  0.]
 [ 0.  0.  0.  1.  1.  1.]
 [ 0.  0.  0.  1.  1.  1.]
 [ 0.  0.  0.  1.  1.  1.]]
```

The main difference between arrays and matrices is in regards to the behavior of the product of two objects of the same type. For example, multiplication between two arrays means "element-wise multiplication of the entries of the two arrays", and requires two objects of the same shape.

```
>>> a=numpy.array([[1,2],[3,4]])
>>> a*a
array([[ 1,   4],
       [ 9, 16]])
```

On the other hand, matrix multiplication requires a first matrix with shape (m, n), and a second matrix with shape (n, p) — the number of columns in the first matrix must be the same as the number of rows in the second matrix. This operation offers a new matrix of shape (m, p), as shown in the following diagram:

$$\begin{pmatrix} 1 & 2 \\ 3 & 4 \end{pmatrix} \cdot \begin{pmatrix} 1 & 2 \\ 3 & 4 \end{pmatrix} = \begin{pmatrix} 7 & 10 \\ 15 & 22 \end{pmatrix}$$

The following is the code snippet:

```
>>> A=numpy.mat(a)
>>> A*A
matrix([[ 7, 10],
        [15, 22]])
```

If we desire to perform an element-wise multiplication of the elements of two matrices, we may do so with the versatile numpy.multiply command, as follows:

```
>>> numpy.multiply(A,A)
matrix([[ 1,   4],
        [ 9, 16]])
```

The other notable difference between arrays and matrices is in regards to their shapes. While we allow one-dimensional arrays, their corresponding matrices must have two dimensions. This is very important to have in mind when we transpose either object.

```
>>> a=numpy.arange(5); A=numpy.mat(a)
>>> a.shape, A.shape, a.transpose().shape, A.transpose().shape
((5,), (1, 5), (5,), (5, 1))
```

SciPy extends the basic applications that we access by offering interesting matrix creation commands, and many related methods. It also allows us the opportunity to speed up computations in the cases where special matrices are used.

The `scipy.linalg` module allows the creation of the special matrices such as, block diagonal matrices from provided arrays (`block_diag`), circulant matrices (`circulant`), companion matrices (`companion`), Hadamard matrices (`hadamard`), Hankel matrices (`hankel`), Hilbert and inverse Hilbert matrices (`hilbert`, `invhilbert`), Leslie matrices (`leslie`), square Pascal matrices (`pascal`), Toeplitz matrices (`toeplitz`), and lower-triangular matrices (`tri`).

Let's see an example on optimal weightings.

Suppose we are given p objects to be weighed in n weighings with a two-pan balance. We create an n x p matrix of plus-minus ones, where a positive value in the position (i, j) indicates that the jth object is placed in the left pan of the balance in the ith weighing, and a negative value indicates that the jth object is placed in the right pan of the balance in the ith weighing.

It is known that optimal weighings are designed by submatrices of Hadamard matrices. For the problem of designing an optimal weighing for eight objects with three weighings, we could then explore different choices of three rows of a Hadamard matrix of order eight. The only requirement is that the sum of the elements on the row of the matrix is zero (so that the same number of objects is placed on each pan). With some smart slicing, we can accomplish just that:

```
>>> A=scipy.linalg.hadamard(8)
>>> zero_sum_rows = (numpy.sum(A,0)==0)
>>> B=A[zero_sum_rows,:]
>>> print B[0:3,:]
[[ 1 -1  1 -1  1 -1  1 -1]
 [ 1  1 -1 -1  1  1 -1 -1]
 [ 1 -1 -1  1  1 -1 -1  1]]
```

The `scipy.sparse` module has its own set of special matrices. The most common are matrices of ones along diagonals (`eye`), identity matrices (`identity`), matrices from diagonals (`diags`, `spdiags`), block diagonal matrices from sparse matrices (`block_diag`), matrices from sparse sub-blocks (`bmat`), column-wise and row-wise stacks (`hstack`, `vstack`), and random matrices of given shape and density with uniformly distributed values (`rand`).

Matrix methods

Besides inheriting all the array methods, matrices enjoy four extra attributes – T for transpose, H for conjugate transpose, I for inverse, and A to cast as `ndarray`.

```
>>> A = numpy.matrix("1+1j, 2-1j; 3-1j, 4+1j")
>>> print A.T; print A.H
[[ 1.+1.j   3.-1.j]
 [ 2.-1.j   4.+1.j]]
[[ 1.-1.j   3.+1.j]
 [ 2.+1.j   4.-1.j]]
```

Operations between matrices

We have briefly covered the most basic operation between two matrices, the matrix product. For any other kind of product we resort to the basic utilities in the NumPy libraries – dot product for arrays or vectors (`dot`, `vdot`), inner and outer products of two arrays (`inner`, `outer`), tensor dot product along specified axes (`tensordot`), or the Kronecker product of two arrays (`kron`).

Let's see an example on creation of orthonormal bases.

Create an orthonormal basis of the nine-dimensional real space from an orthonormal basis of the three-dimensional real space.

For example, we choose the orthonormal basis formed by the vectors.

$$
\begin{aligned}
v_1 &= \tfrac{1}{\sqrt{2}}(1,0,1), \\
v_2 &= (0,1,0), \\
v_3 &= \tfrac{1}{\sqrt{2}}(1,0,-1)
\end{aligned}
$$

We compute the desired basis by collecting these vectors in a matrix and using a Kronecker product, as follows:

```
>>> mu=1/numpy.sqrt(2)
>>> A=numpy.matrix([[mu,0,mu],[0,1,0],[mu,0,-mu]])
>>> B=scipy.linalg.kron(A,A)
```

The columns of the matrix B shown previously, give us an orthonormal basis directly. For instance, the vectors with odd indices would be the columns of the following submatrix:

```
>>> print B[:,0:-1:2]
[[ 0.5   0.5   0.    0.5]
 [ 0.    0.    0.    0. ]
 [ 0.5  -0.5   0.    0.5]
 [ 0.    0.    0.    0. ]
 [ 0.    0.    1.    0. ]
 [ 0.   -0.    0.    0. ]
 [ 0.5   0.5   0.   -0.5]
 [ 0.    0.    0.   -0. ]
 [ 0.5  -0.5   0.   -0.5]]
```

Functions on matrices

The `scipy.linalg` module offers a useful set of functions on matrices. The basic two commands on square matrices are `inv` (for the inverse of a matrix) and `det` (for the determinant). The power of a square matrix is given by the normal exponentiation; that is, if A is a square matrix, then `A**2` indicates the matrix product `A*A`.

```
>>> A=numpy.matrix("1,1j;21,3")
>>> print A**2; print numpy.asarray(A)**2
[[-1.+0.j   0.+4.j]
 [ 0.+8.j   7.+0.j]]
[[ 1.+0.j  -1.+0.j]
 [-4.+0.j   9.+0.j]]
```

More advanced commands compute matrix functions that rely on power series representation of expressions involving matrix powers, such as the matrix exponential (for which there are three possibilities – `expm`, `expm2`, and `expm3`), the matrix logarithm (`logm`), matrix trigonometric functions (`cosm`, `sinm`, `tanm`), matrix hyperbolic trigonometric functions (`coshm`, `sinhm`, `tanhm`), the matrix sign function (`signm`), or the matrix square root (`sqrtm`).

Notice the difference between the application of the normal exponential function on a matrix, and the result of a matrix exponential function. In the former case, we obtain the application of numpy.exp to each entry of the matrix; in the latter, we actually compute the exponential of the matrix following the power series representation:

$$e^A = \sum_{n=0}^{\infty} \frac{1}{n!} A^n$$

The following is the code snippet:

```
>>> a=numpy.arange(0,2*numpy.pi,1.6)
>>> A = scipy.linalg.toeplitz(a)
>>> print A
[[ 0.   1.6  3.2  4.8]
 [ 1.6  0.   1.6  3.2]
 [ 3.2  1.6  0.   1.6]
 [ 4.8  3.2  1.6  0. ]]
>>> print numpy.exp(A)
[[   1.          4.95303242   24.5325302    121.51041752]
 [   4.95303242  1.           4.95303242    24.5325302 ]
 [  24.5325302   4.95303242   1.             4.95303242]
 [ 121.51041752 24.5325302    4.95303242     1.         ]]
>>> print scipy.linalg.expm(A)
[[ 1271.76972856  916.49316549  916.63015271  1271.70874469]
 [  916.49316549  660.86560972  660.5306514    916.63015271]
 [  916.63015271  660.5306514   660.86560972   916.49316549]
 [ 1271.70874469  916.63015271  916.49316549  1271.76972856]]
```

For sparse square matrices, we have an optimized inverse function, as well as a matrix exponential – scipy.sparse.linalg.inv, scipy.sparse.linalg.expm.

For general matrices, we have the basic norm function (norm), as well as two versions of the Moore-Penrose pseudoinverse (pinv and pinv2).

Once again, we need to emphasize how important it is to rely on these functions, rather than coding their equivalent expressions manually. For instance, note the norm computation of vectors or matrices, scipy.linalg.norm. Let us show, by example, the two-norm of a two-dimensional vector v=numpy.matrix([x,y]), where at least one of the x and y values is extremely large—large enough so that x*x overflows.

```
>>> x=10**100; y=9; v=numpy.matrix([x,y])
>>> scipy.linalg.norm(v,2)      # the right method
9.9999999999999982e+99
>>> numpy.sqrt(x*x+y*y)         # the wrong method
Traceback (most recent call last):
  File "<stdin>", line 1, in <module>
AttributeError: sqrt
```

Eigenvalue problems and matrix decompositions

Another set of operations required on matrices is related to the computation and handling of eigenvalues and eigenvectors of square matrices. These two problems rank among the most complex operations that we can perform on square matrices, and extensive research has been put to obtaining good algorithms with low complexity and optimal usage of memory resources. Scipy has state-of-the-art code for implementing these ideas.

For the computation of eigenvalues, the `scipy.linalg` module provides with the three routines, such as `eigvals` (for any ordinary or general eigenvalue problem), `eigvalsh` (if the matrix is symmetric of complex Hermitian), and `eigvals_banded` (if the matrix is banded). To compute the eigenvectors, we also have three corresponding choices – `eig`, `eigh`, and `eigh_banded`.

The syntax in all cases is very similar. For example, for the general case of eigenvalues, we use the following line of code:

```
eigvals(A, B=None, overwrite_a=False)
```

The matrix A must be square, of course. It should be the only parameter passed to the routine if we wish to solve an ordinary eigenvalue problem. If we wish to generalize it, we may provide with an extra square matrix (of the same dimensions as matrix A). This is passed in the B parameter.

The module also offers an extensive collection of functions that compute different decompositions of matrices, as follows:

- **Pivoted LU decomposition**: We can use the `lu` and `lufactor` commands.
- **Singular value decomposition**: We can use the `svd` command. To compute the singular values, we issue `svdvals`. If we wish to compose the sigma matrix in the singular value decomposition from its singular values, we do so with the `diagsvd` routine. If we wish to compute an orthogonal basis for the range of a matrix using SVD, we can do so with the `orth` command.

- **Cholesky decomposition**: We can use `cholesky`, `cholesky_banded`, `cho_factor`.

- **QR and QZ decompositions**: We can use the `qr` and `qz` commands. If we wish to multiply a matrix with the matrix Q of a decomposition, we use the syntactic sugar `qr_multiply`, rather than performing this procedure in two steps.

- **Schur and Hessenberg decompositions**: We can use `schur` and `Hessenberg`. If we wish to convert a real Schur form to complex, we have the `rsf2csf` routine.

At this point we have an interesting application, which makes use of some of the routines explained so far, image compression.

Image compression via the singular value decomposition

This is a very simple application where a square image A of size n x n, stored as `ndarray` is regarded as a matrix, and **singular value decomposition (SVD)** is performed on it.

$$A = U \cdot S \cdot V^*, \quad U = \begin{pmatrix} u_1 \\ \vdots \\ u_n \end{pmatrix}, S = \begin{pmatrix} s_1 & & \\ & \ddots & \\ & & s_n \end{pmatrix}, V^* = \begin{pmatrix} v_1 & \cdots & v_n \end{pmatrix}$$

From all the singular values of s we choose a fraction, together with their corresponding left and right singular vectors u, v. We compute a new matrix by collecting them according to the formula given in the following diagram:

$$\sum_{j=1}^{k} s_j \left(u_j \cdot v_j \right)$$

Note, for example, how much alike are the original (512 singular values) and an approximation using only 32 singular values:

```
import scipy
from scipy.linalg import svd
import matplotlib.pyplot as plt
img=scipy.misc.lena()
U,s,Vh=svd(img)        # Singular Value Decomposition
A = numpy.dot( U[:,0:32],   # use only 32 singular values
```

```
              numpy.dot( numpy.diag(s[0:32]),
                         Vh[0:32,:]))
    plt.subplot(121,aspect='equal'); plt.imshow(img); plt.gray()
    plt.subplot(122,aspect='equal'); plt.imshow(A)
```

This produces the following images, of which the left one is the original image and the right one shows the approximation via 32 singular values:

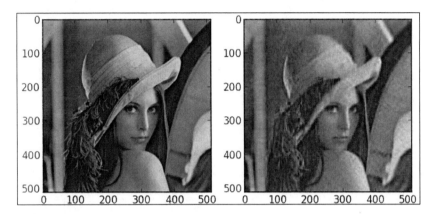

The obvious advantage comes upon the realization that for the full image we need 512 times 512 coefficients (that is 262,144 floating point units), whereas for this approximation via SVD, we only need 32,800 ((2 * 32 * 512) + 32) coefficients. This is one-eighth of the original information.

Solvers

One of the main applications of linear algebra is to the solution of large systems of linear equations. For the basic systems of the form Ax=b, for any square matrix A and a general matrix b (with as many rows as columns in A), we have two generic methods to find x (solve for dense matrices and spsolve for sparse matrices), with the following syntax:

```
solve(A, b, sym_pos=False, lower=False, overwrite_a=False, overwrite_
b=False, debug=False)
spsolve(A, b[, permc_spec, use_umfpack])
```

There are solvers that are more sophisticated in SciPy, with enhanced performance for situations in which the structure of the matrix A is known. For dense matrices we have three commands in the scipy.linalg module – solve_banded (for banded matrices), solveh_banded (if besides banded, A is Hermitian), and solve_triangular (for triangular matrices).

When a solution is not possible (for example, if A is a singular matrix), it is still possible to obtain a matrix x that minimizes the norm of b-Ax in the least-squares sense. We can compute such a matrix with the lstsq command, which has the following syntax:

```
lstsq(A, b, cond=None, overwrite_a=False, overwrite_b=False)
```

The output of this function is a tuple that contains the following:

- The solution found (as ndarray)
- The sum of residues (as another ndarray)
- The effective rank of the matrix A
- The singular values of the matrix A (as another ndarray)

Let us illustrate this routine with a simple example, to solve the following system:

$$\begin{pmatrix} 0 & 1 & 0 \\ 0 & 0 & 1 \\ 0 & 0 & 0 \end{pmatrix} \cdot \begin{pmatrix} x \\ y \\ z \end{pmatrix} = \begin{pmatrix} 1 \\ 2 \\ 3 \end{pmatrix}$$

The following is the code snippet:

```
>>> A=numpy.mat(numpy.eye(3,k=1))
>>> b=numpy.mat(numpy.arange(3)).T
>>> xinfo=scipy.linalg.lstsq(A,b)
>>> print xinfo[0].T        # output the solution
[[ 0.  0.  1.]]
```

The overwrite_ options are designed to enhance performance of the algorithms, and should be used carefully, since they destroy the original data.

The truly fastest solvers coded in SciPy are based upon decomposition of matrices. Reducing the system into something simpler easily solves huge and really complicated systems of linear equations. We may do so at this point using the decompositions presented in the previous section, but of course the SciPy philosophy is to help us deal with all the nuisances of memory and resources internally. We then have the extra solvers coded in this module, such as lu_solve (for solutions based on LU decompositions), and cho_solve, cho_solve_banded (for solutions based on Cholesky decompositions).

There are also solvers for more complex matrix equations – the Sylvester equation (`solve_sylvester`), both the continuous and discrete algebraic Riccati equations (`solve_continuous_are, solve_discrete_are`); and both the continuous and discrete Lyapunov equations (`solve_discrete_lyapunov, solve_lyapunov`).

Most of the matrix decompositions and solutions to eigenvalue problems are contemplated for sparse matrices in the `scipy.sparse.linalg` module, with a similar naming convention but much more robust use of computer resources and error control.

Summary

This chapter explored the treatment of matrices (whether normal or sparse) with the modules on linear algebra – `linalg` and `sparse.linalg`, which expand and improve the NumPy module with the same name.

SciPy for Numerical Analysis

All the different areas of numerical analysis are contemplated in some SciPy module. For example, in order to compute values of special functions we use the `scipy.special` module. The `scipy.interpolate` module takes care of interpolation, extrapolation, and regression. For optimization, we have the `scipy.optimize` module, and finally, for numerical evaluation of integrals, we have the `scipy.integrate` module. This last module serves as the interface to perform numerical solutions of ordinary differential equations as well.

Evaluation of special functions

The `scipy.special` module contains numerically stable definitions of useful functions. We would like to point out that often the straightforward evaluation of a function at a single value is not very efficient. For instance, we would rather use a Horner scheme to find the value of a polynomial at a point, instead of the raw formula. NumPy and SciPy modules ensure that this optimization is always guaranteed with the definition of all its functions, whether by means of Horner schemes or with more advanced techniques.

Convenience and test functions

All the convenience functions are designed to facilitate a computational environment where the user does not need to worry about relative errors. The functions seem to be pointless at first sight, but behind their codes, there are state-of-the-art ideas that offer faster and more reliable results.

We have convenience functions beyond the ones defined in the NumPy libraries to deal with trigonometric functions in degrees (`cosdg`, `sindg`, `tandg`, `cotdg`); to compute angles in radians from their expressions in degrees, minutes and seconds (`radian`); common powers (`exp2` for $2^{**}x$, and `exp10` for $10^{**}x$); and common functions for small values of the variable (`log1p` for $log(1 + x)$, `expm1` for $exp(x)-1$, and `cosm1` for $cos(x)-1$).

For instance, in the following code snippet, the `log1p` function computes the natural logarithm of *1 + x*. Why not simply add 1 to the value of *x*, and then take the logarithm instead? Let us compare:

```
>>> a=scipy.special.exp10(-16)
>>> numpy.log(1+a)
0.0
>>> scipy.special.log1p(a)
9.9999999999999998e-17
```

While the absolute error of the first computation is small, the relative error is 100 percent.

In the same way as Lena image is regarded as the performance test in image processing, we have a few functions that are used to test different algorithms in different scenarios. For instance, it is customary to test minimization codes against the Rosenbrock's banana function:

$$f(x, y) = (1 - x^2) + 100(y - x^2)^2$$

The corresponding optimization module, `scipy.optimize` has a routine to accurately evaluate this function (`rosen`), its derivative (`rosen_der`), its Hessian matrix (`rosen_hess`), or the product of the latter with a vector (`rosen_hess_prod`).

Univariate polynomials

Polynomials are defined in SciPy as a NumPy class, `poly1d`. This class has a handful of methods associated to compute the coefficients of the polynomial (`coeffs` or simply `c`), to compute the roots of the polynomial (`r`), to compute its derivative (`deriv`), to compute the symbolic integral (`integ`), to obtain the degree (`order` or simply `o`), and a method (`variable`) that provides with a string holding the name of the variable used in the proper definition.

In order to define a polynomial, we must indicate either its coefficients or its roots:

```
>>> P1=numpy.poly1d([1,0,1])          # using coefficients
>>> print P1
   2
1 x + 1
```

```
>>> print P1.r; print P1.o; P1.deriv()  # roots,order,derivative
[ 0.+1.j  0.-1.j]
2
poly1d([2, 0])
>>> P2=numpy.poly1d([1,1,1], True)      # using roots
>>> print P2
   3     2
1 x - 3 x + 3 x - 1
```

We may evaluate polynomials by treating them either as (vectorized) functions, or with the __call__ method:

```
>>> P1( numpy.arange(10) )           # evaluate at 0,1,...,9
array([ 1,  2,  5, 10, 17, 26, 37, 50, 65, 82])
>>> P1.__call__(numpy.arange(10))    # same evaluation
array([ 1,  2,  5, 10, 17, 26, 37, 50, 65, 82])
```

There are also a handful of routines associated to polynomials – roots (to compute zeros), polyder (to compute derivatives), polyint (to compute integrals), polyadd (to add polynomials), polysub (to subtract polynomials), polymul (to multiply polynomials), polydiv (to perform polynomial division), polyval (to evaluate polynomials), and polyfit (to compute the best fit polynomial of certain order for two given arrays of data).

The usual binary operators +, -, *, and / perform the corresponding operations with polynomials. In addition, once a polynomial is created, any list of values that interacts with them is immediately casted to a polynomial. Therefore, the following four commands are equivalent:

- numpy.polyadd(P1, numpy.poly1d([2,1]))
- numpy.polyadd(P1, [2,1])
- P1 + numpy.poly1d([2,1])
- P1 + [2,1]

Note how the polynomial division offers both quotient and reminder. For example:

```
>>> P1/[2,1]
(poly1d([ 0.5 , -0.25]), poly1d([ 1.25]))
```

This reads as follows:

$$\underbrace{\frac{x^2 + 1}{2x + 1}}_{} = \underbrace{\left(\frac{1}{2}x - \frac{1}{4}\right)}_{\text{quotient}} + \frac{\overbrace{5/4}^{\text{reminder}}}{2x + 1}$$

A family of polynomials is said to be orthogonal with respect to an inner product if for any two polynomials in the family, their inner product is zero. Sequences of these functions are used as the backbone of extremely fast algorithms of quadrature (for numerical integration of general functions). The `scipy.special` module contains both `poly1d` definitions, and fast evaluation of the families of orthogonal polynomials, such as Legendre (`legendre`), all Chebyshev polynomials (`chebyt`, `chebyu`, `chebyc`, `chebys`), Jacobi (`jacobi`), Laguerre and its generalized version (`laguerre` and `genlaguerre`), Hermite and its normalized version (`hermite` and `hermitenorm`), and Gegenbauer (`gegenbauer`). There are also shifted versions of some of them (`sh_legendre`, `sh_chebyt`, and so on).

The usual evaluation of polynomials can be improved for orthogonal polynomials; thanks to their rich mathematical structure. In these cases, we never evaluate them with the generic call methods presented previously. Instead, we employ the `eval_` syntax. For example, for Jacobi polynomials, we use the following:

```
eval_jacobi(n, alpha, beta, x)
```

In order to obtain the graph of the Jacobi polynomial of order `n = 3`, for `alpha = 0`, `beta = 1`, for a thousand values of x uniformly spaced from `-1` to `1`, we could issue the following command (output not shown):

```
>>> x=numpy.linspace(-1,1,1000)
>>> matplotlib.pyplot.plot(x,eval_jacobi(3,0,1,x))
```

The gamma function

The gamma function is a logarithmic, convex, smooth function operating on complex numbers, which interpolates the factorial function for all nonnegative integers. It is not defined at zero or any negative integer. This is the most common special function, and is widely used in many different applications, either by itself or as the main ingredient in the definition of many other functions. Concrete applications of the gamma function spread to such diverse fields as quantum physics, astrophysics, statistics, or fluid dynamics.

The gamma function is defined by the improper integral, shown as follows:

$$\Gamma(z) = \int_0^\infty e^{-t} t^{z-1}\, dt$$

Evaluation of gamma at integer values gives shifted factorials, and actually, that is precisely how the factorials are coded in SciPy.

The `scipy.special` module has algorithms to obtain fast evaluation of the gamma function at any other permissible values. It also contains routines to perform evaluation of the most common compositions of the gamma functions appearing in the literature – `gammaln` for the natural logarithm of the absolute value of gamma, `rgamma` for the value one over gamma, `beta` for quotients, and `betaln` for the natural logarithm of the latter. We also have implementations of the logarithm of its derivative (`psi`).

An obvious application of gamma functions is the ability to access computations that are virtually impossible for a computer if approached in a direct way. For instance, in statistical applications we often work with ratios of factorials. If these factorials are too large for the precision of the computer, we resort to expressions involving their logarithms instead. But still, computing *ln(a! / b!)* may prove an impossible task (try, for example with *a* = 10**15 and *b* = *a-10**10*). An elegant solution uses the digamma function `psi` by an application of the mean value theorem on the *ln(gamma(x))* function and proper estimation, we obtain the excellent approximation (for this case of choice of *a* and *b*).

$$\ln(a!/b!) \approx 10^{10} \psi(a)$$

The following is the code:

```
>>> 10^10*scipy.special.psi(10**15)
345387763949.10681
```

The Riemann zeta function

Of huge impact in analytic number theory, and with applications to physics and probability theory, we have the Riemann zeta function, which computes *p*-series for any complex value *p*:

$$\zeta(p) = \sum_{n=1}^\infty \frac{1}{n^p}$$

The definition coded in SciPy allows a more flexible generalization of this function, as follows:

$$\texttt{zeta(a,p)} = \sum_{n=0}^{\infty} \frac{1}{(n+a)^p}$$

Airy (and Bairy) functions

These are the solutions to the Stokes equation, as shown in the following diagram:

$$y'' = xy$$

This equation has two linearly independent solutions, both of them defined as an improper integral for real values of the independent variable. The `airy` command computes both functions (`Ai` and `Bi`) as well as their corresponding derivatives (`Aip`, `Bip`). In the following code, we take advantage of the `contourf` command in `matplotlib.pyplot`, to present an image of the real part of the output of the Bairy function `Bi`, for an array of 801 x 801 complex values uniformly spaced in the square from `-4-4j` to `4+4j`. We also offer this graph as a surface plot using the `mplot3d` module of `mpl_toolkits`:

```
import mpl_toolkits.mplot3d
x=numpy.mgrid[-4:4:100j,-4:4:100j]
z=x[0]+1j*x[1]
(Ai, Aip, Bi, Bip) = scipy.special.airy(z)
steps = range(int(Bi.real.min()), int(Bi.real.max()),6)
fig=matplotlib.pyplot.figure()
subplot1=fig.add_subplot(121,aspect='equal')
subplot1.contourf(x[0], x[1], Bi.real, steps)
subplot2=fig.add_subplot(122,projection='3d')
subplot2.plot_surface(x[0],x[1],Bi.real)
```

The output is as follows:

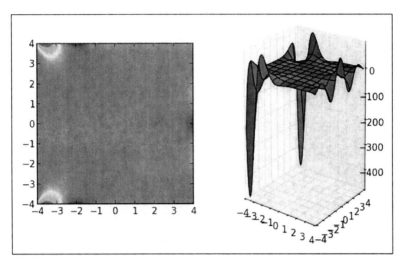

Bessel and Struve functions

Bessel functions are both of the canonical solutions to Bessel's homogeneous differential equations.

$$x^2 y'' + xy' + (x^2 - \alpha^2)y = 0.$$

These equations arise naturally in the solution of Laplace's equation in cylindrical coordinates. The solutions of the non-homogeneous Bessel differential equation shown in the following diagram are called **Struve functions**:

$$x^2 y'' + xy' + (x^2 - \alpha^2)y = \frac{4(x/2)^{\alpha+1}}{\sqrt{\pi}\left(\alpha + \frac{1}{2}\right)}.$$

In either case, the order of the equation is the complex number `alpha`, and acts as a parameter. Depending on the canonical solution and the order, the Bessel and Struve functions are addressed (and computed) differently.

For Bessel functions, we have algorithms to produce the first kind (jv), the second kind (yn, yv), Hankel functions of the first and second kind (hankel1, hankel2), and the modified Bessel functions of the first and second kind (iv, kn, kv). Their syntax is similar in all cases – first parameter is the order, and second parameter the independent variable. n in the definition indicates that an integer is to be used as the order (since they are optimally coded for that situation).

```
>>>scipy.special.jn(5,numpy.pi)
```

```
0.71044976796351567
```

The module also contains fast versions of the most common Bessel functions (those of orders 0 and 1) – j0(x), j1(x) — first kind — y0(x), y1(x) — second kind, and so on. There are definitions of the spherical Bessel functions such as sph_jn(n,z), sph_yn(z); the Riccati-Bessel functions such as riccati_jn(n,x) and riccati_yn(n,x); and derivatives of all the basic ones such as jvp, yvp, kvp, ivp, h1vp, and h2vp.

For Struve functions, we have fast algorithms to compute solutions of the differential equation of order v – (struve(v,x), modstruve(v,x)).

Other special functions

There are more special functions included in this module, of great use in many applications to both pure and applied mathematics. An exhaustive list would be too large for the scope of this chapter, and we encourage exploring the different utilities for each set of special functions. Among the most interesting ones we have elliptic functions, Gauss' hypergeometric functions, parabolic cylinder functions, Mathieu functions, spheroidal wave functions, and Kelvin functions.

Interpolation and regression

Interpolation is a basic method in numerical computation that is obtained from a discrete set of data points, some higher order structure that contains the previous data. The best known example is the interpolation of a sequence of points (x_k, y_k) in a plane to obtain a curve that goes through all the points in the order dictated by the sequence. If the points in the previous sequence are in the right position and order, it is possible to find a univariate function, $y = f(x)$ for which $y\_k = f(x\_k)$. It is often reasonable to request this interpolating function to be a polynomial, or a rational function, or a more complex functional object. Interpolation is also possible in higher dimensions, of course. The objective of the scipy.interpolate module is precisely to offer a complete set of optimally coded applications to address this problem in different settings.

Let us address the most naïve way of interpolating data to obtain a polynomial, Lagrange interpolation. Given a sequence of different x values of size n, and a sequence of arbitrary real values y, of the same size n, we seek a polynomial p(x) of the degree of n-1 at the most that satisfies the n constraints p(x[k])=y[k] for all k from 0 to n-1. The following code illustrates how to obtain a polynomial of degree 9 that interpolates the 10 uniformly spaced values of sine in the interval [-1,1]:

```
import scipy.interpolate
x=numpy.linspace(-1,1,10); xn=numpy.linspace(-1,1,1000)
y=numpy.sin(x)
polynomial=scipy.interpolate.lagrange(x, numpy.sin(x))
matplotlib.pyplot.plot(xn,polynomial(xn),x,y,'or')
```

We will obtain the following plot showing Lagrange interpolation:

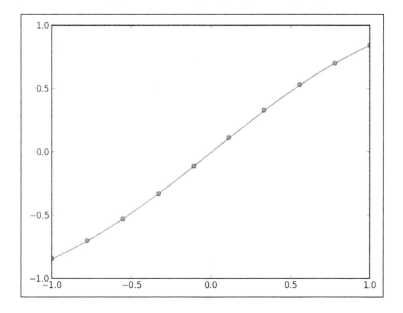

The issues with Lagrange interpolation are numerous. The first obvious drawback arises since the user cannot specify the degree of the interpolation; this depends solely on the data. The procedure is also highly unstable numerically, especially for datasets with sizes over 20 points. This issue can be addressed by allowing the algorithm to depend on different properties of the dataset, rather than just the size and location of the points.

Another inconvenience occurs if we need to update the dataset by adding a few more instances; the procedure needs to be repeated again from the beginning. This proves impractical if the datasets are increasing in size, and the updating is frequent. To address this issue, `BarycentricInterpolator` has the `add_xi` and `set_yi` methods. For example, in the next session we start by interpolating 10 uniformly spaced values of the sine function between 1 and 10. Once done, we update the interpolating polynomial with 10 more uniformly spaced values between 1.5 and 10.5:

```
>>> x=numpy.linspace(1,10,10); y=numpy.sin(x)
>>> Polynomial=scipy.interpolate.BarycentricInterpolator(x,y)
>>> x=numpy.linspace(1.5,10.5,10); y=numpy.sin(x)
>>> Polynomial.add_xi(x,y)
```

It is also possible to interpolate data not only by point location, but also with derivatives at those locations. The `KrogInterpolator` command allows it, by including repeated x values, and indicating on the corresponding y values, the location and successive derivatives in order. For instance, if we desire to construct a polynomial that is zero at the origin, one at x = 1, two at x = 2, and has horizontal tangent lines at each of these three locations, we issue the following commands:

```
x=numpy.array([0,0,1,1,2,2]); y=numpy.aray([0,0,1,0,2,0])
interp=scipy.interpolate.KrogInterpolator(x,y)
xn=numpy.linspace(0,2,20)    # evaluate the polynomial in a larger set
matplotlib.pyplot.plot(x,y,'o',xn,interp(xn),'r')
```

This renders the following graph:

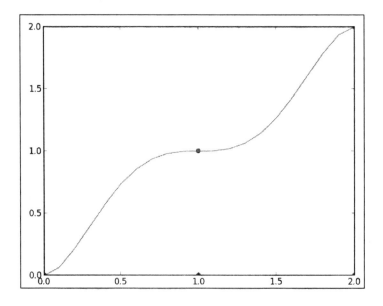

More advanced one-dimensional interpolation is possible with piecewise polynomials (`PiecewisePolynomial`). This allows control over the degrees of different pieces, as well as the derivatives at their intersections. Other interpolation options in the `scipy.interpolate` module are PCHIP monotonic cubic interpolation (pchip), or even univariate splines (`InterpolatedUnivariateSpline`).

Let us examine an example with the latter. Its syntax is as follows:

```
InterpolatedUnivariateSpline(x, y, w=None, bbox=[None, None], k=3)
```

The arrays x and y contain the dependent and independent data, respectively. The array w contains positive weights for spline fitting. The two-sequence bbox specifies the boundary of the approximation interval. The last option indicates the degree of the smoothing polynomials (k).

For instance, we desire to interpolate five points as shown in the following session. These points are ordered by strictly increasing x values. We need to perform this interpolation with four cubic polynomials (one for every two consecutive points), in such a way that at least the first derivative of each two consecutive pieces agree on their intersection. We will proceed as follows:

```
x=numpy.arange(5); y=numpy.sin(x)
xn=numpy.linspace(0,4,40)
interp=scipy.interpolate.InterpolatedUnivariateSpline(x,y)
matplotlib.pyplot.plot(x,y,'.',xn,interp(xn))
```

This offers the following plot showing interpolation with univariate splines:

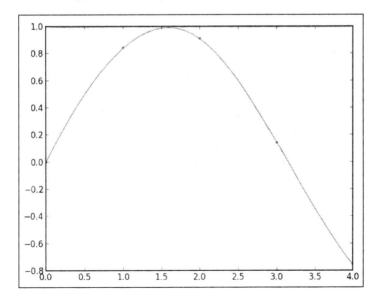

SciPy excels at interpolating in two-dimensional grids as well. It performs well with simple piecewise polynomials (`LinearNDInterpolator`), with piecewise constants (`NearestNDInterpolator`), or with more advanced splines (`BivariateSpline`). It is capable of carrying spline interpolation on rectangular meshes in a plane (`RectBivariateSpline`) or on the surface of a sphere (`RectSphereBivariateSpline`). For unstructured data, besides basic `BivariateSpline`, it is capable of computing smooth approximations (`SmoothBivariateSpline`) or more involved weighted least-squares splines (`LSQBivariateSpline`).

The following code creates a 10 x 10 grid of uniformly spaced points in the square from (0, 0) to (9, 9), and evaluates the function, `sin(x) * cos(y)` on them. We use these points to create a `BivariateSpline`, and evaluate the resulting function on the square for all values.

```
x=y=numpy.arange(10)
f=(lambda i,j: numpy.sin(i)*numpy.cos(j))   # function to interpolate
A=numpy.fromfunction(f, (10,10))            # generate samples
spline=scipy.interpolate.RectBivariateSpline(x,y,A)
fig=matplotlib.pyplot.figure()
subplot=fig.add_subplot(111,projection='3d')
xx=numpy.mgrid[0:9:100j, 0:9:100j]          # larger grid for plotting
A=spline(numpy.linspace(0,9,100), numpy.linspace(0,9,100))
subplot.plot_surface(xx[0],xx[1],A)
```

The output is as follows, which shows interpolation of 2D data with bivariate splines:

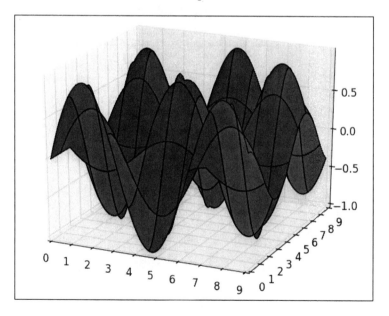

Regression is similar to interpolation. In this case, we assume that the data is imprecise, and we require an object of pre-determined structure to fit the data as closely as possible. The most basic example is univariate polynomial regression to a sequence of points. We obtain that with the `polyfit` command, which we introduced before briefly. For instance, we would like to compute the regression line in the least-squares sense, to a sequence of 10 uniformly spaced points on the interval from 0 to π/2 and their values under the sine function.

```
x=numpy.linspace(0,1,10)
y=numpy.sin(x*numpy.pi/2)
line=numpy.polyfit(x,y,deg=1)
matplotlib.pyplot.plot(x,y,'.'.x,numpy.polyval(line,x),'r')
```

This gives the following plot showing linear regression with `polyfit`:

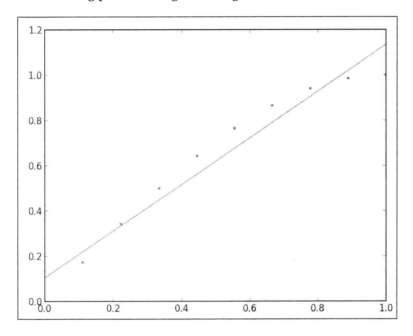

Curve fitting is possible also with splines, by using the parameters wisely. For example, with univariate spline fitting that we introduced before, we can play around with the weights, smoothing factor, the degree of the smoothing spline, and so on. On the same data as the previous example, if we desire to fit to for example, a parabolic spline, we could issue the following code:

```
spline=scipy.interpolate.UnivariateSpline(x,y,k=2)
xn=numpy.linspace(0,1,100)
matplotlib.pyplot.plot(x,y,'.', xn, spline(xn))
```

This gives the following graph showing curve fitting with splines:

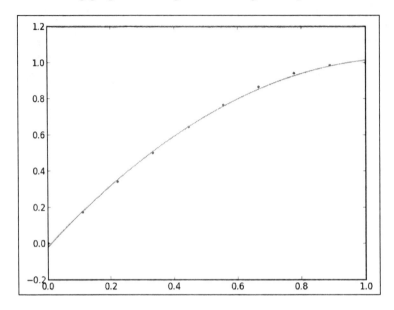

For regression, with the point of view of curve fitting, there is a generic routine, `curve_fit` in the `scipy.optimize` module. This routine minimizes the sum of squares of a set of equations using the Levenberg-Marquardt algorithm, and offers a best fit from any kind of functions (not only polynomials or splines). The syntax is simple as follows:

```
curve_fit(f, xdata, ydata, p0=None, sigma=None, **kw)
```

The `f` parameter is a callable function that represents the function we seek; `xdata` and `ydata` are arrays of the same length, containing the x and y coordinates of the points to be fit. The tuple `p0` holds an initial guess for the values to be found, and `sigma` is a vector of weights that could be used instead of the standard deviation of the data, if needed. We will show its usage with an enlightening example. We will start by generating some points on a section of a sine wave with amplitude `A=18`, angular frequency `w=3π`, and phase `h=0.5`. We corrupt the data in the array `y` with some small noise:

```
A=18; w=3*numpy.pi; h=0.5
x=numpy.linspace(0,1,100); y=A*numpy.sin(w*x+h)
y += 4*((0.5-scipy.rand(100))*numpy.exp(2*scipy.rand(100)**2))
```

We desire now to estimate the values of A, w, and h from the corrupted data, hence technically finding a curve fit from the set of sine waves. We start by gathering the three parameters in a list, and initializing them to some values, say A = 20, w = 2π, and h = 1. We also construct a callable expression of the `target` function:

```
p0 = [20, 2*numpy.pi, 1]
target_function = lambda x,AA,ww,hh: AA*numpy.sin(ww*x+hh)
```

We feed these, together with the fitting data to `curve_fit`, in order to find the required values:

```
pF,pVar = scipy.optimize.curve_fit(target_function, x, y, p0)
```

A sample of `pF` run on any of our experiments should give an accurate result for the three requested values:

```
>>> print pF
[ 18.28142231   9.41943219   0.46405985]
```

This means that A was estimated to about 18.28, w was estimated very close to 3π, and h to about 0.46. The output of the initial data together with a computation of the corresponding sine wave is as follows, in which original data (left, in blue), corrupted (left and right, in red), and computed sine wave (right, in black) are shown:

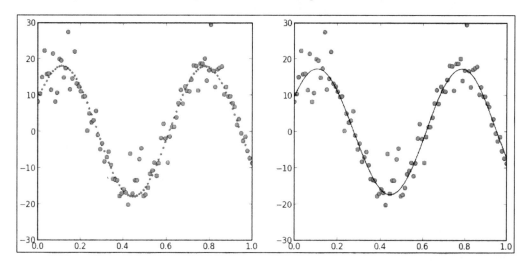

Optimization

The field of optimization deals with finding extreme values of functions or their roots. We have seen the power of optimization already in the curve-fitting arena, but it does not stop here. There are applications to virtually every single branch of engineering, and robust algorithms to perform these tasks are a must in every scientist toolbox.

The `curve_fit` routine is actually syntactic sugar for the general algorithm that performs least-squares minimization – `leastsq`, with the imposing syntax:

```
leastsq(func, x0, args=(), Dfun=None, full_output=0,
        col_deriv=0, ftol=1.49012e-8, xtol=1.49012e-8,
        gtol=0.0, maxfev=0, epsfcn=0.0, factor=100, diag=None):
```

For instance, the `curve_fit` routine could have been called with a `leastsq` call instead:

```
leastsq(error_function,p0,argx=(x,y))
```

Here, `error_function` is equal to `lambda p,x,y: target_function(x,p[0],p[1],p[2])-y`. Most of the optimization routines in SciPy can be accessed from either native Python code, or as wraps of Fortran or C classical implementations of their corresponding algorithms—technically, we are still using the same packages we did under Fortran or C, but from within Python. For instance, the minimization routine that implements the truncated Newton method can be called with `fmin_ncg` (and this is purely Python) or as `fmin_tnc` (and this one is a wrap of a C implementation).

Minimization

For general minimization problems, SciPy has many different algorithms. We have covered so far the least-squares algorithm (`leastsq`), but we also have brute force (`brute`), simulated annealing (`anneal`), Brent or Golden methods for scalar functions (`brent`, `golden`), the downhill simplex algorithm (`fmin`), Powell's method (`fmin_powell`), nonlinear conjugate gradient or Newton's version of it (`fmin_cg`, `fmin_ncg`), and the BFGS algorithm (`fmin_bfgs`).

Constrained minimization is also possible computationally, and SciPy has for this task routines that implement the L-BFGS-S algorithm (`fmin_l_bfgs_s`), truncated Newton's algorithm (`fmin_tnc`), COBYLA (`fmin_cobyla`), or sequential least-squares programming (`fmin_slsqp`).

The following script, for example, compares the output of all different methods to finding a local minimum of the Rosenbrock function, `scipy.optimize.rosen` near the origin, using the downhill simplex algorithm:

```
>>>scipy.optimize.fmin(scipy.optimize.rosen,[0,0])
Optimization terminated successfully.
        Current function value: 0.000000
        Iterations: 79
        Function evaluations: 146
array([ 1.00000439,  1.00001064])
```

Since the 0.11 version of SciPy, all minimization routines can be called from the generic `minimize`, with the `method` parameter pointing to one of the strings such as `Nelder-Mead` (for the downhill simplex), `Powell`, `CG`, `Newton-CG`, `BFGS`, or `anneal`. For constrained minimization, the corresponding strings are one of `L-BFGS-S`, `TNC` (for truncated Newton's), `COBYLA`, or `SLSQP`.

```
minimize( fun, x0, args=(), method='BFGS',
jac=None, hess=None, hessp=None,
         bounds=None, constraints=(),tol=None,
         callback=None, options=None)
```

Roots

For most special functions included in the `scipy.special` module, we have accurate algorithms that allow obtaining their zeros. For instance, for the Bessel function of first kind with integer order, `jn_zeros` offers as many roots as desired (in ascending order). We may obtain the first three roots of the Bessel J-function of order four by issuing the following command:

```
>>> print scipy.special.jn_zeros(4,3)
[   7.58834243   11.06470949   14.37253667]
```

For nonspecial scalar functions, the `scipy.optimize` module allows approximation to the roots through a great deal of different algorithms. For scalar functions, we have the crude bisection method (`bisect`), the classical secant method of Newton-Raphson (`newton`), and more accurate and faster methods such as Ridders' algorithm (`ridder`), and two versions of the Brent method (`brentq` and `brenth`).

The root finding for functions of several variables is very challenging in many ways; the largest the dimension, the worse, of course. The effectiveness of any of these algorithms depends very heavily on the problem, and it is a good idea to invest some time and resources in knowing them all. Since version 0.11 of SciPy, it is possible now to call any of the designed methods with the same routine root, which has the following syntax:

```
root(fun, x0, args=(), method='hybr',
jac=None, tol=None, callback=None, options=None)
```

The different methods are obtained upon changing the value of the method parameter to a method string. We may choose among the methods such as 'hybr' for a modified hybrid Powell's method; 'lm' for a modified least-squares method; 'broyden1' or 'broyden2' for Broyden's good and bad methods, respectively; 'diagbroyden' for diagonal Broyden Jacobian approximation; 'anderson' for Anderson's extended mixing; 'Krylov' for Krylov approximation of the Jacobian; 'linearmixing' for scalar Jacobian approximation; and 'excitingmixing' for a tuned diagonal Jacobian approximation.

For large-scale problems, both the Krylov approximation of the Jacobian or the Anderson extended mixing are usually the best options.

Let us present an illustrative example of the power of these techniques. Consider the following system of differential equations:

$$\begin{cases} x' = x^2 - 2x - y + 0.5 \\ y' = x^2 + 4y^2 - 4 \end{cases}$$

We use the plot routine quiver from the matplotlib.pyplot libraries to visualize a slope field, for values of x and y between -0.5 and 2.5, and hence identify the location of the possible critical points in that region:

```
>>> f=lambda x: [x[0]**2-2*x[0]-x[1]+0.5, x[0]**2-4*x[1]**2-4]
>>>x,y=numpy.mgrid[-0.5:2.5:24j,-0.5:2.5:24j]
>>> U,V=f([x,y])
>>>matplotlib.pyplot.quiver(x,y,U,V,color='r', \
...          linewidths=(0.2,), edgecolors=('k'), \
...          headaxislength=5)
```

This gives the following:

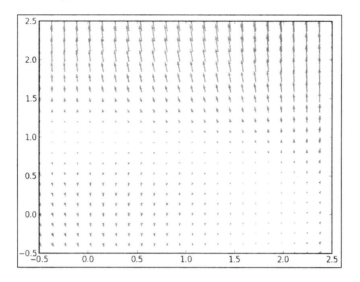

Note how there is a whole region of the plane, in which the slopes are extremely small. Because of the degrees of the polynomials involved, there are at most four different possible critical points. In this area we should be able to identify two (as a matter of fact there are only two noncomplex solutions). One of them seems to be near (0, 1), and the second near (2, 0). We use these two locations as initial guesses for our searches:

```
>>>scipy.optimize.root(f,[0,1])
   status: 1
 success: True
qtf: array([ -4.81190247e-09,  -3.83395899e-09])
nfev: 9
      r: array([ 2.38128242, -0.60840482, -8.35489601])
    fun: array([ 3.59529073e-12,  3.85025345e-12])
      x: array([-0.22221456,  0.99380842])
 message: 'The solution converged.'
fjac: array([[-0.98918813, -0.14665209],
      [ 0.14665209, -0.98918813]])
>>>scipy.optimize.root(f,[2,0])
   status: 1
 success: True
```

```
qtf: array([  2.08960516e-10,   8.61298294e-11])
nfev: 12
   r: array([-4.56575336, -1.67067665, -1.81464307])
 fun: array([  2.44249065e-15,   1.42996726e-13])
   x: array([ 1.90067673,  0.31121857])
message: 'The solution converged.'
fjac: array([[-0.39612596, -0.91819618],
       [ 0.91819618, -0.39612596]])
```

In the first case, we converged successfully to (-0.22221456, 0.99380842). In the second case, we converged to (1.90067673, 0.31121857). The routine informs us details about the convergence and properties of the approximation. For instance, nfev tells us about the number of function calls performed, and fun indicates the output of the function at the found location. The other items in the output reflect the matrices used in the procedure, such as qtf, r, fjac.

Integration

SciPy is capable of performing very robust numerical integration. Definite integrals of a set of special functions are evaluated accurately with routines in the scipy. special module. For other functions, there are several different algorithms to obtain reliable approximations in the scipy.integrate module.

Exponential/logarithm integrals

The next diagram summarizes the indefinite and definite integrals in this category – the exponential integrals – expn, expi, and exp1; Dawson's integral dawsn; and Gauss error functions – erf and erfc. We also have Spence's dilogarithm (also known as Spence's integral).

$$\text{expn(n,x)} = \int_1^\infty \frac{e^{-xt}}{t^n}\,dt \qquad \text{exp1(x)} = \int_1^\infty \frac{e^{-xt}}{t}\,dt$$

$$\text{expi(x)} = \int_{-\infty}^x \frac{e^t}{t}\,dt \qquad \text{dawsn(x)} = e^{-x^2}\int_0^x e^{t^2}\,dt$$

$$\text{erf(x)} = \frac{2}{\sqrt{\pi}}\int_0^x e^{-t^2}\,dt \qquad \text{erfc(x)} = \frac{2}{\sqrt{\pi}}\int_x^\infty e^{-t^2}\,dt$$

$$\text{spence(x)} = -\int_1^x \frac{\log t}{t-1}\,dt$$

Trigonometric and hyperbolic trigonometric integrals

In this category, we have Fresnel sine and cosine integrals, as well as the sinc and hyperbolic trigonometric integrals.

$$\text{fresnel(z)} = \int_0^z \sin\left(\tfrac{\pi}{2}t^2\right) dt$$

$$\text{sici(x)} = \int_0^x \frac{\sin t}{t}\, dt, \quad \gamma + \log x + \int_0^x \frac{\cos t - 1}{t}\, dt$$

$$\text{shichi(x)} = \int_0^x \frac{\sinh t}{t}\, dt, \quad \gamma + \log x + \int_0^x \frac{\cosh t - 1}{t}\, dt$$

In the definitions given in the preceding diagram, gamma denotes the Euler-Mascheroni constant:

$$\gamma = \lim_{n \to \infty}\left(\sum_{k=1}^{n} \frac{1}{k} - \log n\right)$$

Elliptic integrals

These integrals arise naturally when computing the arc length of ellipses. SciPy follows the argument notation for elliptic integrals – complete (one argument) and incomplete (two arguments).

$$\text{ellipkm1(m)} = \int_0^{\pi/2} \frac{d\theta}{\sqrt{1 - m\sin^2\theta}} \qquad \text{ellipe(m)} = \int_0^{\pi/2} \sqrt{1 - m\sin^2\theta}\, d\theta$$

$$\text{ellipkinc(m,n)} = \int_0^n \frac{d\theta}{\sqrt{1 - m\sin^2\theta}} \qquad \text{ellipeinc(m,n)} = \int_0^n \sqrt{1 - m\sin^2\theta}\, d\theta$$

Gamma and beta integrals

The following diagram shows the most useful of them all:

$$\text{gammainc(a,x)} = \frac{1}{\Gamma(a)} \int_0^x e^{-t} t^{a-1}\, dt$$

$$\text{gammaincc(a,x)} = \frac{1}{\Gamma(a)} \int_x^\infty e^{-t} t^{a-1}\, dt$$

$$\text{betainc(a,b,x)} = \frac{\Gamma(a+b)}{\Gamma(a)\Gamma(b)} \int_0^x t^{a-1}(t-1)^{b-1}\, dt$$

Numerical integration

For any other functions, we are content with approximating definite integrals with quadrature formulae, such as quad (adaptive quadrature), fixed_quad (fixed-order Gaussian quadrature), quadrature (fixed-tolerance Gaussian quadrature), and romberg, (Romberg integration). For functions of more than one variable, we have dbquad (two) and tplquad (three). The syntax in all cases is a variation of quad:

```
quad(func, a, b, args=(), full_output=0, epsabs=1.49e-08,
    epsrel=1.49e-08, limit=50, points=None, weight=None,
wvar=None, wopts=None, maxp1=50, limlst=50)
```

If instead of functions we have samples, we may use the routines such as trapz, cumtrapz (composite trapezoidal rule and its cumulative version); romb (Romberg integration again); and simps (Simpson's rule) instead. In these routines the syntax is simpler and changes the order of the parameters; for example, this is how we call simps:

```
simps(y, x=None, dx=1, axis=-1, even='avg')
```

Those of us familiar with the QUADPACK libraries will find similar syntax, usage, and performance.

For extra information, run the scipy.integrate.quad_explain() command. This explains with great detail all the different outputs of the quadrature integrals included in the module result, estimate of absolute error, convergence, and explanation of the used weightings, if necessary. Let us give at least one meaningful example, where we integrate a special function, and compare the output of a quadrature formula against the more accurate value of the routines given in scipy.special:

```
>>> f=lambda t: numpy.exp(-t)*t**4
>>> from scipy.special import gammainc
```

```
>>> from scipy.integrate import quad
>>> from scipy.misc import factorial
>>> print gammainc(5,1)
0.0036598468273437131
>>>result,error=quad(f,0,1)/factorial(4)
>>> result
0.0036598468273437122
```

To use a routine that integrates from samples, we have the flexibility of assigning the frequency and length of the data. For the following problem, we could try with `10,000` samples in the same interval:

```
>>> x=numpy.linspace(0,1,10000)
>>>scipy.integrate.simps(f(x)/factorial(4), x)
0.003659846827346905
```

Ordinary differential equations

As with integration, SciPy has some extremely accurate general-purpose solvers for systems of ordinary differential equations of first order.

$$\frac{d\boldsymbol{y}}{dt} = f(t, \boldsymbol{y}), \quad \boldsymbol{y}(t) = \big(y_1(t), \ldots, y_n(t)\big), t \in \mathbb{R}$$

For the case of real-valued functions we have basically two flavors – ode (with options passed with the `set_integrator` method) and odeint (simpler interface). The syntax of ode is as follows:

```
ode(f,jac=None)
```

The first parameter, `f`, is the function to be integrated, and the second parameter, `jac`, refers to the matrix of partial derivatives with respect to the dependent variables (the Jacobian). This creates an ode object, with different methods to indicate the algorithm to solve the system (`set_integrator`), the initial conditions (`set_initial_value`), and different parameters to be sent to the function or its Jacobian.

The options for integration algorithm are `'vode'` for real-valued variable coefficient ODE solver, with fixed-leading-coefficient implementation (it provides Adam's method for non-stiff problems, and BDF for stiff); `'zvode'` for complex-valued variable coefficient ODE solver, with similar options to the previous; `'dopri5'` for a Runge-Kutta method of order (4)5; `'dop853'` for a Runge-Kutta method of order 8(5, 3).

The next session presents an example of usage of ode to solve the initial value problem:

$$y' = -20y, \quad y(0) = 1$$

We compute each step sequentially, and compare it with the actual solution, which is known. Notice that virtually there is no difference:

```
from scipy.integrate import ode
f=lambda t,y: -20*y          # The ODE
actual_solution=lambda t:numpy.exp(-20*t)  # actual solution
dt=0.01             # time step
solver=ode(f).set_integrator('dop853')  # solver
solver.set_initial_value(1,0)      # initial value
while solver.successful() and solver.t<=1+dt:
    # solve the equation at succesive time steps,
    # until the time is greater than 1
    # but make sure that the solution is successful
    print solver.t, solver.y, actual_solution(solver.t)
    # We compare each numerical solution with the actual
    # solution of the ODE
solver.integrate(solver.t + dt)     # solve next step
```

Once run, this code gives us the following output:

```
<scipy.integrate._ode.ode at 0x10eac5e50>
0 [ 1.] 1.0
0.01 [ 0.81873075] 0.818730753078
0.02 [ 0.67032005] 0.670320046036
0.03 [ 0.54881164] 0.548811636094
0.04 [ 0.44932896] 0.449328964117
0.05 [ 0.36787944] 0.367879441171
0.06 [ 0.30119421] 0.301194211912
0.07 [ 0.24659696] 0.246596963942
0.08 [ 0.20189652] 0.201896517995
0.09 [ 0.16529889] 0.165298888222
0.1 [ 0.13533528] 0.135335283237

    ...
```

```
0.9  [  1.52299797e-08]  1.52299797447e-08
0.91 [  1.24692528e-08]  1.24692527858e-08
0.92 [  1.02089607e-08]  1.02089607236e-08
0.93 [  8.35839010e-09]  8.35839010137e-09
0.94 [  6.84327102e-09]  6.84327102222e-09
0.95 [  5.60279644e-09]  5.60279643754e-09
0.96 [  4.58718175e-09]  4.58718174665e-09
0.97 [  3.75566677e-09]  3.75566676594e-09
0.98 [  3.07487988e-09]  3.07487987959e-09
0.99 [  2.51749872e-09]  2.51749871944e-09
1.0  [  2.06115362e-09]  2.06115362244e-09
```

For systems of differential equations of first order with complex-valued functions, we have a wrapper of `ode`, which we call with the `complex_ode` command. Syntax and usage are similar to those of `ode`.

The syntax of `odeint` is much more intuitive, and more Python friendly:

```
odeint(func, y0, t, args=(), Dfun=None, col_deriv=0, full_output=0,
       ml=None, mu=None, rtol=None, atol=None, tcrit=None, h0=0.0,
hmax=0.0, hmin=0.0, ixpr=0, mxstep=0, mxhnil=0, mxordn=12,
mxords=5, printmessg=0)
```

The most impressive part of this routine is that one is able to indicate not only the Jacobian, but also whether this is banded (and how many nonzero diagonals under or over the main diagonal we have, with the `ml` and `mu` options). This speeds up computations by a huge factor. Another amazing feature of `odeint` is the possibility to indicate critical points for the integration (`tcrit`).

We will now introduce an application to analyze Lorentz attractors with the routines presented in this section.

Lorenz Attractors

No book on scientific computing is complete without revisiting Lorenz attractors; SciPy excels both at computation of solutions and presentation of ideas based upon systems of differential equations, of course, and we show how and why in this section.

Consider a two-dimensional fluid cell that is heated from underneath and cooled from above, much like what occurs with the earth's atmosphere. This creates convection that can be modeled by a single partial differential equation, for which a decent approximation has the form of the following system of ordinary differential equations:

$$\begin{cases} \frac{dx}{dt} = \sigma(y - x) \\ \frac{dy}{dt} = rx - y - xz \\ \frac{dz}{dt} = xy - bz \end{cases}$$

The variable x represents the rate of convective overturning. Variables y and z stand for the horizontal and vertical temperature variations, respectively. This system depends on four physical parameters, the descriptions of which are far beyond the scope of this book. The important point is that we may model earth's atmosphere with these equations, and in that case a good choice for the parameters is given by sigma = 10, and b = 8 / 3. For certain values of the third parameter, we have systems for which the solutions behave chaotically. Let us explore this effect with the help of SciPy.

We will use one of the solvers in the `scipy.integrate` module, as well as plotting utilities:

```
import numpy
from numpy import linspace
import scipy
from scipy.integrate import odeint
import matplotlib.pyplot as plt
from mpl_toolkits.mplot3d import Axes3D
sigma=10.0
b=8/3.0
r=28.0
f = lambda x,t: [sigma*(x[1]-x[0]),
                r*x[0]-x[1]-x[1]*x[2],
                x[0]*x[1]-b*x[2]]
```

Let us choose a time interval t large enough with a sufficiently dense partition and any initial condition, y0.

```
>>> t=linspace(0,20,2000); y0=[5.0,5.0,5.0]
>>> solution=odeint(f,y0,t)
>>> X=solution[:,0]; Y=solution[:,1]; Z=solution[:,2]
```

If we desire to plot a 3D rendering of the solution obtained, we may do so as follows:

```
>>> plt.gca(projection='3d'); plt.plot(X,Y,Z)
```

This produces the following graph, showing a Lorenz attractor:

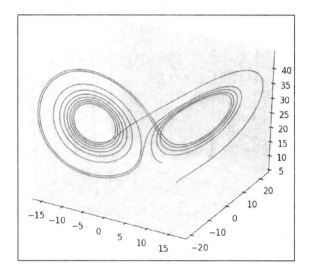

This is most illustrative, and shows precisely the chaotic behavior of the solutions. Let us observe the fluctuations of the vertical temperature in detail, as well as the fluctuation of horizontal temperature against vertical:

```
>>>plt.subplot(121,aspect='equal'); plt.plot(t,Z)
>>>plt.subplot(122,aspect='equal'); plt.plot(Y,Z)
```

This produces the following the plots, showing vertical temperature with respect to time (left) and horizontal versus vertical temperature (right):

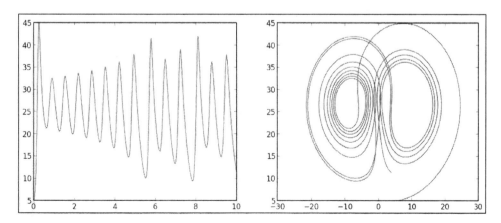

Summary

This chapter explored the topics of special functions, integration, interpolation, and optimization through the corresponding modules (`special`, `integrate`, `interpolate`, `optimize`).

5
SciPy for Signal Processing

We define a signal as data that measures either time-varying or spatially varying phenomena. Sound or electrocardiograms are excellent examples of time-varying quantities, while images embody the quintessential spatially varying cases. Moving images are treated with the techniques of both types of signal, obviously.

The field of signal processing treats four aspects of this kind of data – its acquisition, quality improvement, compression, and feature extraction. SciPy has many routines to treat effectively tasks in any of the four fields. All these are included in two low-level modules (`scipy.signal` being the main one, with an emphasis in time-varying data, and `scipy.ndimage`, for images). Many of the routines in these two modules are based on Discrete Fourier Transform of the data. SciPy has an extensive package of applications and definitions of these background algorithms – `scipy.fftpack`, which we will start covering first.

Discrete Fourier Transforms

The **Discrete Fourier Transform** (**DFT** from now on) transforms any signal from its time/space domain into a related signal in frequency domain. This allows us not only to be able to analyze the different frequencies of the data, but also faster filtering operations, when used properly. It is possible to turn a signal in frequency domain back to its time/spatial domain; thanks to the Inverse Fourier Transform. We will not go into detail of the mathematics behind these operators, since we assume familiarity at some level with this theory. We will focus on syntax and applications instead.

The basic routines in the `scipy.fftpack` module compute the DFT and its inverse, for discrete signals in any dimension – `fft`, `ifft` (one dimension); `fft2`, `ifft2` (two dimensions); `fftn`, `ifftn` (any number of dimensions). All of these routines assume that the data is complex valued. If we know beforehand that a particular dataset is actually real valued, and should offer real-valued frequencies, we use `rfft` and `irfft` instead, for a faster algorithm. All these routines are designed so that composition with their inverses always yields the identity. The syntax is the same in all cases, as follows:

```
fft(x[, n, axis, overwrite_x])
```

The first parameter, x, is always the signal in any array-like form. Note that `fft` performs one-dimensional transforms. This means in particular, that if x happens to be two-dimensional for example, `fft` will output another two-dimensional array where each row is the transform of each row of the original. We can change it to columns instead, with the optional parameter, `axis`. The rest of parameters are also optional; n indicates the length of the transform, and `overwrite_x` gets rid of the original data to save memory and resources. We usually play with the integer n when we need to pad the signal with zeros, or truncate it. For higher dimension, n is substituted by `shape` (a tuple), and `axis` by `axes` (another tuple).

To better understand the output, it is often useful to shift the zero frequencies to the center of the output arrays with `fftshift`. The inverse of this operation, `ifftshift`, is also included in the module. The following code shows some of these routines in action, when applied to a checkerboard image:

```
from scipy.fftpack import fft,fft2, fftshift
import matplotlib.pyplot as plt
B=numpy.ones((4,4)); W=numpy.zeros((4,4))
signal = numpy.bmat("B,W;W,B")
onedimfft = fft(signal,n=16)
twodimfft = fft2(signal,shape=(16,16))
plt.figure()
plt.gray()
plt.subplot(121,aspect='equal')
plt.pcolormesh(onedimfft.real)
plt.colorbar(orientation='horizontal')
plt.subplot(122,aspect='equal')
plt.pcolormesh(fftshift(twodimfft.real))
plt.colorbar(orientation='horizontal')
```

Note how the first four rows of the one-dimensional transform are equal (and so are the last four), while the two-dimensional transform (once shifted) presents a peak at the origin, and nice symmetries in the frequency domain.

In the following screenshot, the left-hand side image is `fft` and right one is `fft2` of a 2 x 2 checkerboard signal:

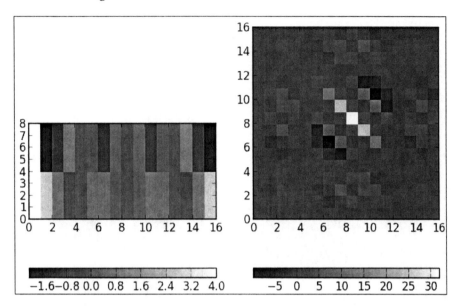

The `scipy.fftpack` module also offers the Discrete Cosine Transform with its inverse (`dct`, `idct`) as well as many differential and pseudo-differential operators defined in terms of all these transforms – `diff` (for derivative/integral); `hilbert`, `ihilbert` (for the Hilbert transform); `tilbert`, `itilbert` (for the h-Tilbert transform of periodic sequences); and so on.

Signal construction

To aid in the construction of signals with predetermined properties, the `scipy.signal` module has a nice collection of the most frequent one-dimensional waveforms in the literature – `chirp` and `sweep_poly` (for the frequency-swept cosine generator), `gausspulse` (a Gaussian modulated sinusoid), `sawtooth` and `square` (for the waveforms with those names). They all take as their main parameter a one-dimensional `ndarray` representing the times at which the signal is to be evaluated. Other parameters control the design of the signal, according to frequency or time constraints.

```
from scipy.signal import chirp, sawtooth, square, gausspulse
import matplotlib.pyplot as plt
t=numpy.linspace(-1,1,1000)
plt.subplot(221); plt.ylim([-2,2])
```

```
plt.plot(t,chirp(t,f0=100,t1=0.5,f1=200))      # plot a chirp
plt.subplot(222); plt.ylim([-2,2])
plt.plot(t,gausspulse(t,fc=10,bw=0.5))         # Gauss pulse
plt.subplot(223); plt.ylim([-2,2])
t*=3*numpy.pi
plt.plot(t,sawtooth(t))                        # sawtooth
plt.subplot(224); plt.ylim([-2,2])
plt.plot(t,square(t))                          # Square wave
```

The following diagram shows waveforms for `chirp` (upper-left), `gausspulse` (upper-right), `sawtooth` (lower-left), and `square` (lower-right):

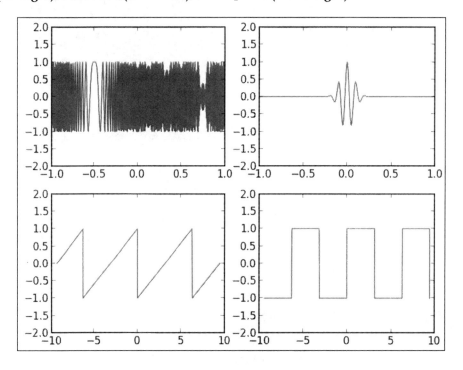

The usual method of creating signals is to import them from file. This is possible by using purely NumPy routines, for example `fromfile`:

```
fromfile(file, dtype=float, count=-1, sep='')
```

The `file` argument may point to either a file or a string, the `count` argument is used to determine the number of items to read, and `sep` indicates what constitutes a separator in the original file/string. For images, we have the versatile routine, `imreadin` in either the `scipy.ndimage` or `scipy.misc` module:

```
imread(fname, flatten=False)
```

The `fname` argument is a string containing the location of an image. The routine infers the type of file, and reads the data into array accordingly. In case if the `flatten` argument is turned to `True`, the image is converted to gray scale. Note that, in order to work, the **Python Imaging Library** (**PIL**) needs to be installed.

It is also possible to load `.wav` files for analysis, with the `read` and `write` routines from the `wavfile` submodule in the `scipy.io` module. For instance, given any audio file with this format, say `audio.wav`, the command, `>>>rate,data = scipy.io.wavfile.read("audio.wav")` assigns an integer value to the `rate` variable, indicating the sample rate of the file (in samples per second), and a NumPy `ndarray` to the `data` variable, containing the numerical values assigned to the different notes. If we wish to write some one-dimensional ndarray `data` into an audio file of this kind, with the sample rate given by the `rate` variable, we may do so by issuing the following command:

```
>>>scipy.io.wavfile.write("filename.wav",rate,data)
```

Filters

A filter is an operation on signals that either removes features or extracts some component. SciPy has a very complete set of known filters, as well as the tools to allow construction of new ones. The complete list of filters in SciPy is long, and we encourage the reader to explore the help documents of the `scipy.signal` and `scipy.ndimage` modules for the complete picture. We will introduce in these pages, as an exposition, some of the most used filters in the treatment of audio or image processing.

We start by creating a signal worth filtering:

```
from numpy import sin, cos, pi, linspace
f=lambda t: cos(pi*t) + 0.2*sin(5*pi*t+0.1) + 0.2*sin(30*pi*t) +
            0.1*sin(32*pi*t+0.1) + 0.1*sin(47* pi*t+0.8)
t=linspace(0,4,400); signal=f(t)
```

We test first the classical smoothing filter of Wiener and Kolmogorov, `wiener`. We present in a plot the original signal (in black) and the corresponding filtered data, with a choice of Wiener window of size 55 samples (in blue). Next we compare the result of applying the median filter, `medfilt` with a kernel of the same size as before (in red):

```
from scipy.signal import wiener, medfilt
plt.plot(t,signal,'k')
plt.plot(t,wiener(signal,mysize=55),'b',linewidth=3)
plt.plot(t,medfilt(signal,kernel_size=55),'r',linewidth=3)
```

This gives us the following graph showing the comparison of smoothing filters (`wiener` is the one that has its starting point just below 0.5 and `medfilt` has its starting point just above 0.5):

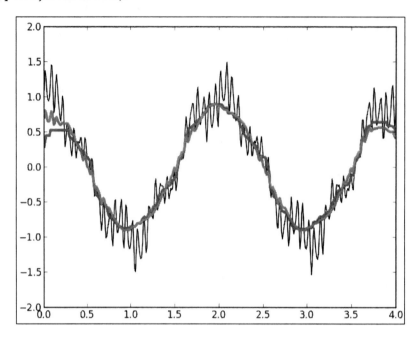

Most of the filters in the `scipy.signal` module can be adapted to work in arrays of any dimension. But in the particular case of images, we prefer to use the implementations in the `scipy.ndimage` module, since they are coded with these objects in mind. For instance, to perform a median filter on an image for smoothing, we use `scipy.ndimage.median_filter`. Let us show an example. We will start by loading Lena to array, and corrupting the image with Gaussian noise (zero mean and standard deviation of 16):

```
from scipy.stats import norm      # Gaussian distribution
lena=scipy.misc.lena().astype(float)
lena+=norm(loc=0,scale=16).rvs(lena.shape)
denoised_lena = scipy.ndimage.median_filter(lena)
```

The set of filters for images come in two flavors – statistical and morphological. For example, among the filters of statistical nature, we have the Sobel algorithm oriented to detection of edges (singularities along curves). Its syntax is as follows:

```
sobel(image, axis=-1, output=None, mode='reflect', cval=0.0)
```

The optional parameter, `axis` indicates the dimension in which the computations are performed. By default, this is always the last axis (-1). The `mode` parameter, which is one of the strings `'reflect'`, `'constant'`, `'nearest'`, `'mirror'`, or `'wrap'`, indicates how to handle the border of the image, in case there is insufficient data to perform the computations there. In case if `mode` is `'constant'`, we may indicate the value to use in the border, with the `cval` parameter.

```
lena=scipy.misc.lena()
sblX=sobel(lena,axis=0); sblY=sobel(lena,axis=1)
sbl=numpy.hypot(sblX,sblY)
```

The following screenshot illustrates the previous two filters in action—Lena (upper-left), noisy Lena (upper-right), edge map with sobel (lower-left), and median filter (lower-right):

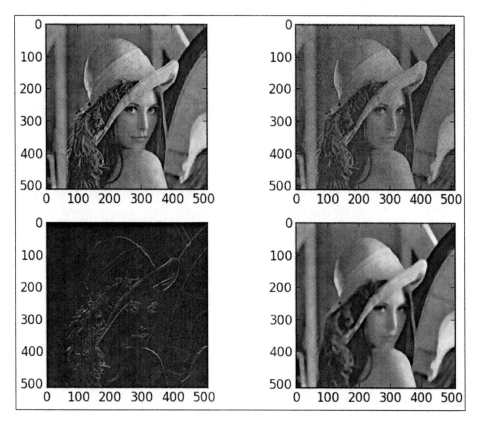

LTI system theory

To investigate the response of a time-invariant linear system to input signals, we have many resources in the `scipy.signal` module. As a matter of fact, to simplify representation of objects, we have a `lti` class (linear-time invariant class) with associated methods such as `bode` (to calculate bode magnitude and phase data), `impulse`, `output`, and `step`.

No matter whether we are working with continuous or discrete-time linear systems, we have routines to simulate such systems (`lsim` and `lsim2` for continuous, `dsim` for discrete), as well as compute impulses (`impulse` and `impulse2` for continuous, `dimpulse` for discrete) and steps (`step` and `step2` for continuous, `dstep` for discrete).

Transforming a system from continuous to discrete is possible with `cont2discrete`, but in either case we are able to provide for any system with any of its representations, as well to convert from one to another. For instance, if we have the zeros z, poles p, and system gain k of the transfer function, we may obtain the polynomial representation (numerator first, then denominator) with `zpk2tf(z,p,k)`. If we have numerator (`num`) and denominator (`dem`) of the transfer function, we obtain the state-space with `tf2ss(num,dem)`. This operation is reversible, with the `ss2tf` routine. The change of representation from zero-pole-gain to/from state-space is also contemplated in the (`zpk2ss`, `ss2zpk`) module.

Filter design

There are routines in the `scipy.signal` module that allow the creation of different kinds of filters with diverse methods. For instance, the `bilinear` routine returns a digital filter from an analog using a bilinear transform. **Finite impulse response (FIR** for short) filters can be designed by the window method with the `firwin` and `firwin2` routines. **Infinite impulse response (IIR** for short) filters can be designed in two different ways, via `iirdesign` or `iirfilter`. Butterworth filters can be designed with the `butter` routine. There are also routines to design filters of Chebyshev (`cheby1`, `cheby2`), Cauer (`ellip`), and Bessel (`bessel`).

Window functions

And no signal processing computational system would be complete without an extensive list of windows—mathematical functions that are zero valued outside specific domains. In this section, we will use a few of the windows coded in the `scipy.signal` module to design very simple smoothing filters by convolution. We will be testing them on the same one-dimensional signal we employed before, for comparison.

We will start by showing the plot of four well-known window functions – Boxcar, Hamming, Blackman-Harris (Nuttall version), and triangular. We will use a size of 31 samples:

```
from scipy.signal import boxcar, hamming, nuttall, triang
windows=['boxcar', 'hamming', 'nuttall', 'triang']
for w in windows:
eval( 'plt.plot(' + w + '(31))' )
plt.ylim([-0.5,2]); plt.xlim([-1,32])
plt.legend(windows)
```

We need to extend the original signal by fifteen samples for plotting purposes:

```
extended_signal=numpy.r_[signal[15:0:-1],signal,signal[-1:-15:-1]]
plt.plot(extended_signal,'k')
```

The final step is the filter itself, which we perform by a simple convolution:

```
for w in windows:
    window = eval( w+'(31)')
    output=numpy.convolve(window/window.sum(),signal)
plt.plot(output,linewidth=2)
plt.ylim([-2,3]); plt.legend(['original'+windows)
```

This produces the following output showing convolution of a signal with different windows:

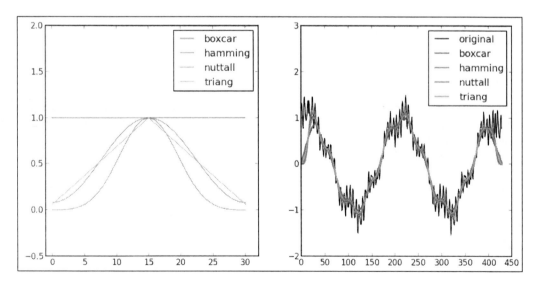

Image interpolation

The set of filters on images that perform some geometric manipulation of the input is classically termed image interpolation, since this numerical technique is the root of all the algorithms. As a matter of fact, SciPy collects all these under the submodule `scipy.ndimage.interpolation` for ease of access. This section is best explained through examples, going over the most meaningful routines for geometric transformation. The starting point is the image Lena. We now assume that all functions from the submodule have been imported into the session.

We need to apply an affine transformation on the domain of the image, given in matrix form as follows:

$$L(x,y) = \underbrace{\begin{pmatrix} a_{11} & a_{12} \\ a_{21} & a_{22} \end{pmatrix}}_{A} \begin{pmatrix} x \\ y \end{pmatrix} + \underbrace{\begin{pmatrix} b_1 \\ b_2 \end{pmatrix}}_{b}$$

To apply the transformation on the domain of the image we will issue the `affine_transform` command (note the syntax is self explanatory):

```
A=numpy.mat("0,1;-1,1.25"); b=[-400,0]
Ab_Lena=affine_transform(lena,A,b,output_shape=(512*2.2,512*2.2))
```

For a general transformation, we use the `geometric_transform` routine with the following syntax:

```
geometric_transform(input, mapping, output_shape=None,
                    output=None, order=3, mode='constant',
cval=0.0, prefilter=True, extra_arguments=(),
extra_keywords={})
```

We need to provide a rank-2 map from tuples to tuples as the parameter mapping. For instance, we desired to apply the Möbius transform for complex-valued number z (where we assume the values of a, b, c, and d are already defined and they are complex-valued numbers).

$$f(z) = \frac{az + b}{cz + d}$$

We would have to code it in the following way:

```
def f(z):
    temp = a*(z[0]+1j*z[1]) + b
    temp /= c*(z[0]+1j*z[1])+d
    return (temp.real, temp.imag)
```

In both functions, the values of the grid that cannot be computed directly with the formula are inferred with spline interpolation. We may specify the order of this interpolation with the `order` parameter. The points outside the domain of definition are not interpolated, but filled according to some predetermined rule. We may impose this rule by passing a string to the `mode` option. The choices are – `'constant'`, to use a constant value that we may impose with the `cval` option; `'nearest'`, that continues the last value of the interpolation on each level line; `'reflect'` or `'wrap'`, which are self explanatory.

For example, for the values `a = 2**15*(1+1j)`, `b = 0`, `c = -2**8*(1-1j*2)`, and `d = 2**18-1j*2**14`, we obtain (after imposing the `reflect` mode) the result, as shown just after this line of code:

```
Moebius_Lena = geometric_transform(lena,f,mode='reflect')
```

The following screenshot shows affine transformation (left) and geometric transformation (right):

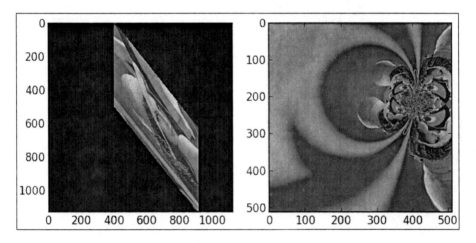

For the special cases of rotations, shifts, or dilations, we have the syntactic sugar routines `rotate(input,angle)`, `shift(input, offset)`, and `zoom(input,dilation_factor)`.

Given any image, we know the value of the array at pixel values (with integer coordinates) in the domain. But, what would be the corresponding value of a location without integer coordinates? We may obtain that information with the valuable routine, `map_coordinates`. Note that the syntax may be confusing, especially with the parameter coordinates:

```
map_coordinates(input, coordinates, output=None, order=3,
                mode='constant', cval=0.0, prefilter=True)
```

For instance, if we wish to evaluate Lena at the locations (10.5, 11.7) and (12.3, 1.4), we collect the coordinates as a sequence of sequences; the first internal sequence contains the x values, and the second, the y values. We may specify the order of splines used with `order`, and the interpolation scheme outside of the domain, if needed, as in the previous examples.

```
>>>lena=scipy.misc.lena().astype(float)
>>> coordinates=[[10.5, 12.3], [11.7, 1.4]]
>>>map_coordinates(lena, coordinates, order=1)
array([ 157.2 ,  157.42])
>>>map_coordinates(lena, coordinates, order=2)
array([ 157.80641507,  157.6741489 ])
```

Morphology

We also have the possibility of creating and applying filters to images based on mathematical morphology, both to binary and gray-scale images. The four basic morphological operations are opening (`binary_opening`), closing (`binary_closing`), dilation (`binary_dilation`), and erosion (`binary_erosion`). Note that the syntax for each of these filters is very simple, since we only need two ingredients – the signal to filter and the structuring element to perform the morphological operation.

```
binary_operation(signal, structuring_element)
```

We have illustrated the use some of these operations towards an application to obtain the structural model of an oxide, but we postpone this example until we cover the notions of triangulations and Voronoi diagrams in *Chapter 7, SciPy for Computational Geometry*.

We may use combinations of these four basic morphological operations to create more complex filters for removal of holes, hit-or-miss transforms (to find the location of specific patterns in binary images), denoising, edge detection, and many more. The module even provides with some of the most common filters constructed this way. For instance, for the location of the letter "e" in a text (which we covered previously as an application of correlation), we could use the following command instead:

```
>>>binary_hit_or_miss(text, letterE)
```

For gray-scale images, we may use a structuring element or a footprint. The syntax is, therefore, a little different:

```
grey_operation(signal, [structuring_element, footprint, size, ...])
```

If we desire to use a completely flat and rectangular structuring element (all ones), then it is enough to indicate the size as a tuple. For instance, to perform gray-scale dilation of a flat element of size `(15,15)` on our classical image of Lena, we issue the following command:

```
>>>grey_dilation(lena, size=(15,15))
```

The last kind of morphological operations coded in the `scipy.ndimage` module perform distance and feature transforms. Distance transforms create a map that assigns to each pixel the distance to the nearest object. Feature transforms provide with the index of the closest background element instead. These operations are used to decompose images into different labels. We may even choose different metrics such as Euclidean distance, chessboard distance, and taxicab distance. The syntax for the distance transform using a brute force algorithm is as follows:

```
distance_transform_bf(signal, metric='euclidean', sampling=None,
    return_distances=True, return_indices=False,
                    distances=None, indices=None)
```

We indicate the metric with the strings such as `'euclidean'`, `'taxicab'`, or `'chessboard'`. If we desire to provide the feature transform instead, we switch `return_distances` to `False` and `return_indices` to `True`.

Similar routines are available with more sophisticated algorithms – `distance_transform_cdt` (using chamfering for taxicab and chessboard distances). For Euclidean distance, we also have `distance_transform_edt`. All these use the same syntax.

Summary

In this chapter we explored signal processing (any dimensional) including the treatment of signals in frequency space, by means of their Discrete Fourier Transforms. These correspond to the `fftpack`, `signal`, and `ndimage` modules.

6
SciPy for Data Mining

This section deals with those branches of mathematics that treat the collection, organization, analysis, and interpretation of data. The different applications and operations spread over several modules and submodules – `scipy.stats` (for purely statistical tools), `scipy.ndimage.measurements` (for analysis and organization of data), `scipy.spatial` (for spatial algorithms and data structures), and finally the clustering package `scipy.cluster`, with its two submodules – `scipy.cluster.vq` (vector quantization) and `scipy.cluster.hierarchy` (for hierarchical and agglomerative clustering).

Descriptive statistics

We often require the analysis of data in which certain features are grouped in different regions, each with different sizes, values, shapes, and so on. The `scipy.ndimage.measurements` submodule has the right tools for this task, and the best way to illustrate the capabilities of the module is by means of an exhaustive examples. For example, for binary images of zeros and ones, it is possible to label each blob (areas of contiguous pixels with value one) and obtain the number of these with the `label` command. If we desire to obtain the center of mass of the blobs, we may do so with the `center_of_mass` command. We may see these operations in action once again in the application to obtaining the structural model of oxides in next chapter.

For nonbinary data, the `scipy.ndimage.measurements` submodule provides with the usual basic statistical measurements (value and location of extreme values, mean, standard deviation, sum, variance, histogram, and so on).

For more advanced statistical measurements we must access functions from the `scipy.stats` module. We may now use geometric and harmonic means (`gmean`, `hmean`), median, mode, skewness, various moments, or kurtosis (`median`, `mode`, `skew`, `moment`, `kurtosis`). For an overview of the most significant statistical properties of the dataset, we prefer to use the `describe` routine. We may also compute item frequencies (`itemfreq`), percentiles (`scoreatpercentile`, `percentileofscore`), histograms (`histogram`, `histogram2`), cumulative and relative frequencies (`cumfreq`, `relfreq`), standard error (`sem`), and the signal-to-noise ratio (`signaltonoise`), which is always useful.

Distributions

One of the main strengths of the `scipy.stats` module is the great number of distributions coded, both continuous and discrete. The list is impressively large and has 81 continuous distributions and 10 discrete distributions.

One of the most usual ways to employ these distributions is the generation of random numbers. We have been employing this technique to "contaminate" our images with noise, for example:

```
>>> from scipy.stats import norm     # Gaussian distribution
>>>lena=scipy.misc.lena().astype(float)
>>>lena+= norm.rvs(loc=0,scale=16,size=lena.shape)
>>>signaltonoise(lena,axis=None)
array(2.4578546916065163)
```

Let's see the SciPy way of handling distributions. First, a random variable class is created (in SciPy there is the `rv_continuous` class for continuous random variables, and the `rv_discrete` class for the discrete case). Each continuous random variable has associated a probability density function (`pdf`), a cumulative distribution function (`cdf`), a survival function along with its inverse (`sf`, `isf`), and all possible descriptive statistics. They also have associated the random variable per se, `rvs`, which is what we used to actually generate the random instances. For example, with a Pareto continuous random variable with parameter $b = 5$, to check these properties, we could issue the following:

```
>>> from scipy.stats import pareto
>>> import matplotlib.pyplot as plt
>>> x=numpy.linspace(1,10,1000)
>>>plt.subplot(131); plt.plot(pareto.pdf(x,5))
>>>plt.subplot(132); plt.plot(pareto.cdf(x,5))
>>>plt.subplot(133); plt.plot(pareto.rvs(5,size=1000))
```

This gives the following graphs showing probability density function (left), cumulative distribution function (center), and random generation (right):

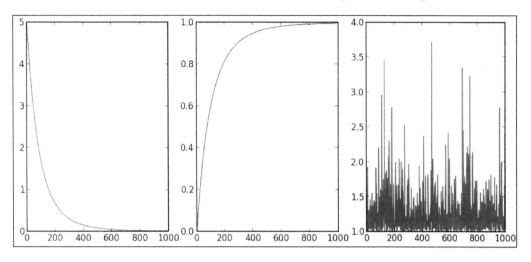

Interval estimation, correlation measures, and statistical tests

We briefly covered interval estimation as an introductory example of SciPy – `bayes_mvs`, in *Chapter 1, Introduction to SciPy*, with very simple syntax, as follows:

```
bayes_mvs(data, alpha=0.9)
```

It offers a tuple of three arguments, in which each argument has the form `(center, (lower, upper))`. The first argument refers to the mean, the second refers to the variance, and the third to the standard deviation. All intervals are computed according to the probability given by `alpha`, which is `0.9` by default.

We may use the `linregress` routine to compute the regression line of some two-dimensional data x, or two sets of one-dimensional data, x and y. We may compute different correlation coefficients, with their corresponding p-values, as well. We have the Pearson correlation coefficient (`pearsonr`), Spearman's rank-order correlation (`spearmanr`), point biserial correlation (`pointbiserialr`), and Kendall's tau for ordinal data (`kendalltau`). In all cases, the syntax is the same, as it is only required either a two-dimensional array of data, or two one-dimensional arrays of data with the same length.

SciPy also has most of the best-known statistical tests and procedures – t-tests (`ttest_1samp` for one group of scores, `ttest_ind` for two independent samples of scores, or `ttest_rel` for two related samples of scores), Kolmogorov-Smirnov tests for goodness of fit (`kstest`, `ks_2samp`), one-way Chi-square test (`chisquare`), and many more.

Let us illustrate some of the routines of this module with a textbook example, based on Timothy Sturm's studies on control design.

Twenty-five right-handed individuals were asked to use their right hands to turn a knob that moved an indicator by screw action. There were two identical instruments, one with a right-handed thread where the knob turned clockwise, and the other with a left-hand thread where the knob turned counter-clockwise. The following table gives the times in seconds each subject took to move the indicator to a fixed distance.

Subject	1	2	3	4	5	6	7	8	9	10
Right thread	113	105	130	101	138	118	87	116	75	96
Left thread	137	105	133	108	115	170	103	145	78	107
Subject	11	12	13	14	15	16	17	18	19	20
Right thread	122	103	116	107	118	103	111	104	111	89
Left thread	84	148	147	87	166	146	123	135	112	93
Subject	21	22	23	24	25					
Right thread	78	100	89	85	88					
Left thread	76	116	78	101	123					

We may perform an analysis that leads to a conclusion about right-handed people finding right-hand threads easier to use, by a simple one-sample t-statistic. We will load the data in memory, as follows:

```
>>> data = numpy.array([[113,105,130,101,138,118,87,116,75,96, \
... 122,103,116,107,118,103,111,104,111,89,78,100,89,85,88], \
... [137,105,133,108,115,170,103,145,78,107, \
... 84,148,147,87,166,146,123,135,112,93,76,116,78,101,123]])
```

The difference of each row indicates which knob was faster, and for how much time. We can obtain that information easily, and perform some basic statistical analysis on it. We will start by computing the mean, standard deviation, and a histogram with 10 bins:

```
>>>dataDiff = data[1,:]-data[0,:]
>>>dataDiff.mean(), dataDiff.std()
(13.720000000000001, 21.62872164507186)
```

```
>>>matplotlib.pyplot.hist(dataDiff)
(array([2, 1, 1, 5, 3, 4, 1, 4, 1, 3]),
 array([-28.,-20.,-12.,-4.,4.,12.,20.,28.,36.,44.,52.]),
<a list of 10 Patch objects>)
```

The following histogram is produced:

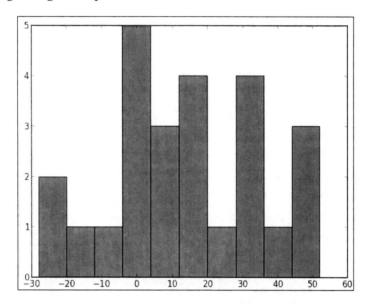

Under the light of this histogram, it is not too far fetched to assume a normal distribution. If we assume that this is a proper simple random sample, the use of t-statistics is justified. We would like to prove that it takes longer to turn the left thread than the right, so we set the mean of dataDiff to be contrasted against the zero mean (which would indicate that it takes the same time for both threads). The two-sample t-statistics and p-value for the two-sided test are computed by the simple command, as follows:

```
>>>t_stat,p_value=ttest_1samp(dataDiff)
```

The p-value for the one-sided test is then calculated:

```
>>> print p_value/2.0
0.00239943063239
```

Note that this p-value is much smaller than either of the usual thresholds alpha = 0.05 or alpha = 0.1. We can thus guarantee that we have enough evidence to support the claim that right-handed threads take less time to turn than left-handed threads.

Distribution fitting

In Timothy Sturm's example we claim that the histogram of some data seemed to fit a normal distribution. SciPy has a few routines to help us approximate the best distribution to a random variable, together with the parameters that best approximate this fit. For example, for the data in that problem, the mean and standard deviation of the normal distribution that realizes the best fit can be found in the following way:

```
>>>mean,std=norm.fit(dataDiff)
```

We can now plot the (normed) histogram of the data, together with the computed probability density function, as follows:

```
>>>matplotlib.pyplot.hist(dataDiff, normed=1)
(array([ 0.01,0.005,0.005,0.025,0.015,0.02,0.005,0.02,
        0.005,  0.015]),
 array([-28.,-20.,-12.,-4.,4.,12.,20.,28.,36.,44.,52.]),
<a list of 10 Patch objects>)
>>> x=numpy.linspace(dataDiff.min(),dataDiff.max(),1000)
>>>pdf=norm.pdf(x,mean,std)
>>>matplotlib.pyplot.plot(x,pdf)
```

We will obtain the following graph showing the maximum likelihood estimate to the normal distribution that best fits `dataDiff`:

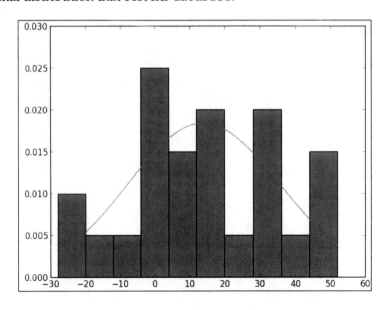

We may even fit the best probability density function without specifying any particular distribution, thanks to a non-parametric technique, kernel density estimation. We can find an algorithm to perform Gaussian kernel density estimation in the `scipy.stats.kde` submodule. Let us show by example with the same data as before:

```
>>> from scipy.stats.ked import gaussian_kde
>>>pdf=Gaussian_kde(dataDiff)
```

A similar plotting session as before, offers us the following graph, showing probability density function obtained by kernel density estimation on `dataDiff`:

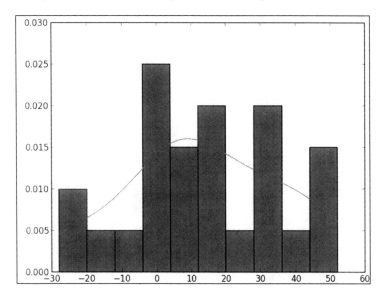

Distances

In the field of data mining, it is often required to determine which members of a training set are closest to unknown test instances. It is imperative to have a good set of different distance functions for any of the algorithms that perform the search, and SciPy has for this purpose a huge collection of optimally coded functions in the `distance` submoduleof the `scipy.spatial` module. The list is long. Besides Euclidean, squared Euclidean, or standardized Euclidean, we have many more – Bray-Curtis, Canberra, Chebyshev, Manhattan, correlation distance, cosine distance, dice dissimilarity, Hamming, Jaccard-Needham, Kulsinski, Mahalanobis, and so on. The syntax in most cases is simple:

```
distance_function(first_vector, second_vector)
```

The only three cases in which the syntax is different are the Minkowski, Mahalanobis, and standarized Euclidean distances, in which the distance function requires either an integer number (for the order of the norm in the definition of Minkowski distance), a covariance for the Mahalanobis case (but this is an optional requirement), or a variance matrix to standardize the Euclidean distance.

Let us see now a fun exercise to visualize the unit balls in Minkowski metrics:

```
Square=numpy.meshgrid[-1.1:1.1:512j,-1.1,1.1:512j]
X=Square[0]; Y=Square[1]
f=lambda x,y,p: minkowski([x,y],[0.0,0.0],p)<=1.0
Ball=lambda p:numpy.vectorize(f)(X,Y,p)
```

We have created a function `Ball`, which creates a grid of 512 x 512 Boolean values. The grid represents a square of length 2.2 centered at the origin, with sides parallel to the coordinate axis, and the true values on it represent all those points of the grid inside of the unit ball for the Minkowksi metric, for the parameter `p`. All we have to do is show it graphically, like in the following example:

```
>>>matplotlib.pyplot.imshow(Ball(3)); plt.axis('off')
```

This produces the following, where `Ball(3)` is a unit ball in the Minkowski metric with parameter `p = 3`:

We feel the need to issue the following four important warnings:

- **First warning**: We must use these routines, instead of creating our own definitions of the corresponding distance functions whenever possible. They guarantee a faster result, and optimal coding to take care of situations in which the inputs are either too large or too small.

- **Second warning**: These functions work great when comparing two vectors; however, for the pairwise computation of many vectors, we must resort to the pdist routine. This command takes an *m x n* array representing *m* vectors of dimension *n*, and computes the distance of each of them to each other. We indicate the distance function to be used with the option metric, and additional parameters as needed. For example, for the Manhattan (cityblock) distance for five randomly selected four-dimensional vectors with integer values 1, 0, or -1, we could issue the following command:

```
>>> V=scipy.stats.randint.rvs(0.4,3,size=(5,4))-1
>>> print V
[[ 1  0  1 -1]
 [-1  0 -1  0]
 [ 1  1  1 -1]
 [ 1  1 -1  0]
 [ 0  0  1 -1]]
>>>pdist(V,metric='cityblock')
array([ 5.,  1.,  4.,  1.,  6.,  3.,  4.,  3.,  2.,  5.])
```

This means, if v1 = [1,0,1,-1], v2 = [-1,0,-1,0], v3 = [1,1,1,-1], v4 = [1,1,-1,0], and v5 = [0,0,1,-1], then the Manhattan distance of v1 from v2 is 5. The distance from v1 to v3 is 1; from v1 to v4 is 4; from v1 to v5 is 1. From v2 to v3 the distance is 6; from v2 to v4 is 3; from v2 to v5 is 4. From v3 to v4 the distance is 3; from v3 to v5 is 2. And finally, the distance from v4 to v5 is 5, which is the last entry of the output.

- **Third warning**: When computing the distance between each pair of two collections of inputs, we use the cdist routine, which has a similar syntax. For instance, for the two collections of three randomly selected four-dimensional Boolean vectors, the corresponding Jaccard-Needham dissimilarities are computed, as follows:

```
>>> V=scipy.stats.randint.rvs(0.4,2.size=(3,4)).astype(bool)
>>> W=scipy.stats.randint.rvs(0.4,3.size=(3,4)).astype(bool)
>>>cdist(V,W,'jaccard')
array([[ 0.75      ,  1.        ],
       [ 0.75      ,  1.        ],
       [ 0.33333333,  0.5       ]])
```

That is, if the three vectors in V are labeled v1 through v3 and if the two vectors in W are labeled as w1 and w2, then the dissimilarity between v1 and w1 is 0.75; between v1 and w2 is 1; and so on.

- **Fourth warning**: When we have a large amount of data points, and we need to address the problem of nearest neighbors (for example, to locate the closest element of the data to a new instance point), we seldom do it by brute force. The optimal algorithm to perform this search is based in the idea of k-dimensional trees. SciPy has two classes to handle these objects – KDTree and cKDTree. The latter is a subset of the former, a little faster since it is wrapped from C code, but with very limited use. It only has the query method to find the nearest neighbors of the input. The syntax is simple, as follows:

```
KDTree(data, leafsize=10)
```

This creates a structure containing a binary tree, very apt for the design of fast search algorithms. The leafsize option indicates at what level the search based on the structure of binary tree must be abandoned in favor of brute force.

The other methods associated to the KDTree class are – count_neighbors, to compute the number of nearby pairs that can be formed with another KDTree; query_ball_point, to find all points at a given distance from the input; query_ball_tree and query_pairs, to find all pairs of points within certain distance; and sparse_distance_matrix, that computes a sparse matrix with the distances between two KDTree classes.

Let us see it in action, with a small dataset of 10 randomly generated four-dimensional points with integer entries:

```
>>> data=scipy.stats.randint.rvs(0.4,10,size=(10,4))
>>> print data
[[8 6 1 1]
 [2 9 1 5]
 [4 8 8 9]
 [2 6 6 4]
 [4 1 2 1]
 [3 8 7 2]
 [1 1 3 6]
 [5 2 1 5]
 [2 5 7 3]
 [6 0 6 9]]
>>> tree=KDTree(data)
>>>tree.query([0,0,0,0])
(4.6904157598234297, 4)
```

This means, among all the points in the dataset, the closest one in the Euclidean distance to the origin is the fifth one (index 4), and the distance is precisely about 4.6 units.

We may input more than one point; the output will still be a tuple, where the first entry is an array that indicates the smallest distance to each of the input points. The second entry is another array that indicates the indices of the nearest neighbors.

Clustering

Another technique used in data mining is clustering. SciPy has two modules to deal with any problem in this field, each of them addressing a different clustering tool – `scipy.cluster.vq` for k-means and `scipy.cluster.hierarchy` for hierarchical clustering.

Vector quantization and k-means

We have two routines to divide data into clusters using the k-means technique – `kmeans` and `kmeans2`. They correspond to two different implementations. The former has a very simple syntax:

```
kmeans(obs, k_or_guess, iter=20, thresh=1e-05)
```

The `obs` parameter is an `ndarray` with the data we wish to cluster. If the dimensions of the array are $m \times n$, the algorithm interprets this data as m points in the n-dimensional Euclidean space. If we know the number of clusters in which this data should be divided, we input so with the `k_or_guess` option. The output is a tuple with two elements. The first is an `ndarray` of dimension $k \times n$, representing a collection of points — as many as clusters were indicated. Each of these locations indicates the centroid of the found clusters. The second entry of the tuple is a floating-point value indicating the distortion between the passed points, and the centroids generated previously.

If we wish to impose an initial guess for the centroids of the clusters, we may do so with the `k_or_guess` parameter again, by sending a $k \times n$ `ndarray`.

The data we pass to `kmeans` need to be normalized with the `whiten` routine.

The second option is much more flexible, as its syntax indicates:

```
kmeans2(data, k, iter=10, thresh=1e-05,
minit='random', missing='warn')
```

The `data` and `k` parameters are the same as `obs` and `k_or_guess`, respectively. The difference in this routine is the possibility of choosing among different initialization algorithms, hence providing us with the possibility to speed up process and use fewer resources if we know some properties of our data. We do so by passing to the `minit` parameter one of the strings such as `'random'` (initialization centroids are constructed randomly using a Gaussian), `'points'` (initialization is done by choosing points belonging to our data), or `'uniform'` (if we prefer uniform distribution to Gaussian).

In case we would like to provide the initialization centroids ourselves with the `k` parameter, we must indicate our choice to the algorithm by passing `'matrix'` to the `minit` option as well.

In any case, if we wish to classify the original data by assigning to each point the cluster to which it belongs; we do so with the `vq` routine (for vector quantization). The syntax is pretty simple as well:

```
vq(obs, centroids)
```

The output is a tuple with two entries. The first entry is a one-dimensional `ndarray` of size *n* holding for each point in `obs`, the cluster to which it belongs. The second entry is another one-dimensional `ndarray` of same size, but containing floating-point values indicating the distance from each point to the centroid of its cluster.

Let us illustrate with a classical example, the mouse dataset. We will create a big dataset with randomly generated points in three disks, as follows:

```
>>> from scipy.stats import norm
>>> from numpy import array,vstack
>>> data=norm.rvs(0,0.3,size=(10000,2))
>>>inside_ball=numpy.hypot(data[:,0],data[:,1])<1.0
>>> data=data[inside_ball]
>>> data = vstack((data, data+array([1,1]),data+array([-1,1])))
```

Once created, we request the data to be separated into three clusters:

```
>>> from scipy.cluster.vq import *
>>> centroids, distortion = kmeans(data,3)
>>>cluster_assignment, distances = vq(data,centroids)
```

Let us present the results:

```
>>> from matplotlib.pyplot import plot
>>> plot(data[cluster_assignment==0,0], \
```

```
...        data[cluster_assignment==0,1], 'r.')
[<matplotlib.lines.Line2D at 0x10b84ad50>]
>>> plot(data[cluster_assignment==1,0], \
...        data[cluster_assignment==1,1], 'b.')
[<matplotlib.lines.Line2D at 0x10b84af50>]
>>> plot(data[cluster_assignment==2,0], \
...        data[cluster_assignment==2,1], 'k.')
[<matplotlib.lines.Line2D at 0x10b84e8d0>]
```

This gives the following plot showing the mouse dataset with three clusters from left to right – red (0), blue (1), and black (2):

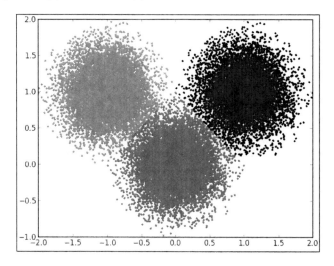

Hierarchical clustering

There are several different algorithms to perform hierarchical clustering. SciPy has routines for the following methods:

- **Single/min/nearest method**: `single`
- **Complete/max/farthest method**: `complete`
- **Average/UPGMA method**: `average`
- **Weighted/WPGMA method**: `weighted`
- **Centroid/UPGMC method**: `centroid`
- **Median/WPGMC method**: `median`
- **Ward's linkage method**: `ward`

In any of the previous cases, the syntax is the same; the only input is the dataset, which can be either an *m x n* `ndarray` representing *m* points in the *n*-dimensional Euclidean space, or a condensed distance matrix obtained from the previous data using the `pdist` routine from `scipy.spatial`. The output is always an `ndarray` representing the corresponding linkage matrix of the clustering obtained.

Alternatively, we may call the clustering with the generic routine, `linkage`. This routine accepts a dataset/distance matrix, and a string indicating the method to use. The strings coincide with the names introduced before. The advantage of `linkage` over the previous routines is that we are also allowed to indicate a different metric than the usual Euclidean distance. The complete syntax for `linkage` is then as follows:

```
linkage(data, method='single', metric='euclidean')
```

Different statistics on the resulting linkage matrices may be performed with the routines such as Cophenetic distances between observations (`cophenet`); inconsistency statistics (`inconsistent`); maximum inconsistency coefficient for each non-singleton cluster with its descendants (`maxdists`); and maximum statistic for each non-singleton cluster with its descendants (`maxRstat`).

It is customary to use binary trees to represent linkage matrices, and the `scipy.cluster.hierachy` submodule has a large number of different routines to manipulate and extract information from these trees. The most useful of these routines is the visualization of these trees, often called dendrograms. The corresponding routine in SciPy is dendrogram, and has the following imposing syntax:

```
dendrogram(Z, p=30, truncate_mode=None, color_threshold=None,
get_leaves=True, orientation='top', labels=None,
count_sort=False, distance_sort=False,
show_leaf_counts=True, no_plot=False, no_labels=False,
color_list=None, leaf_font_size=None,
leaf_rotation=None, leaf_label_func=None,
no_leaves=False, show_contracted=False,
link_color_func=None)
```

The first obvious parameter, Z, is a linkage matrix. This is the only non-optional variable. The other options control the style of the output (colors, labels, rotation, and so on), and since they are technically nonmathematical in nature, we will not explore them in detail in this monograph, other than through the simple application to animal clustering shown next.

Clustering mammals by their dentition – Mammal's teeth are divided into four groups such as incisors, canines, premolars, and molars. The dentition of several mammals has been collected, and is available for download at www.uni-koeln.de/themen/statistik/data/cluster/dentitio.dat.

This file presents the name of the mammal, together with the number of top incisors, bottom incisors, top canines, bottom canines, top premolars, bottom premolars, top molars, and bottom molars.

We wish to use hierarchical clustering on that dataset to assess which species are closer to each other by these features.

We start by preparing the dataset and store the relevant data in ndarrays. The original data is given as a text file, where each line represents a different mammal. The first four lines are as follows:

```
OPOSSUM                      54113344
HAIRY TAIL MOLE              33114433
COMMON MOLE                 32103333
STAR NOSE MOLE              33114433
```

The first twenty-seven characters of each line hold the name on the animal. The characters in positions twenty-eight to thirty-five are the number of respective kind of denture. We need to prepare this data into something that SciPy can handle. We collect the names apart, since we will be using them as labels in the dendrogram. The rest of the data will be forced into an array of integers:

```
file=open("dentitio.dat","r")     # open the file
lines=file.readlines()         # read each line in memory
file.close()          # close the file
mammals=[]                    # this stores the names
dataset=numpy.zeros((len(list),8))  # this stores the data
for index,line in enumerate(lines):
mammals.append( line[0:27].rstrip(" ").capitalize() )
    for tooth in range(8):
        dataset[index,tooth]=int(line[27+tooth])
```

We proceed to compute the linkage matrix and its posterior dendrogram, making sure to use the Python list mammals as labels:

```
>>> from scipy.cluster.hierachy import linkage, dendrogram
>>> Z=linkage(dataset)
>>>dendrogram(Z, labels=mammals, orientation="right")
>>>matplotlib.pyplot.show()
```

This gives us the following dendrogram showing clustering of mammals according to their dentition:

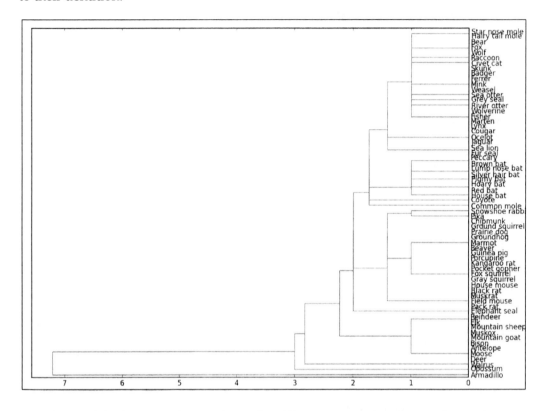

Note how all the bats are clustered together. The mice are also clustered together, but far from the bats. Sheep, goats, antelopes, deer, and moose have similar dentures too, and they appear clustered at the bottom of the tree, next to the opossum and the armadillo. Note how all felines are also clustered together, on the top of the tree.

Experts in data analysis can obtain more information from dendrograms; they are able to interpret the lengths of the branches or the different colors used in the composition, and give us more insightful explanations about the way the clusters differ from each other.

Summary

This chapter dealt with tools appropriate for data mining, and explored the modules such as `stats` (for statistics), `spatial` (for data structures), and `cluster` (for clustering and vector quantization).

7
SciPy for Computational Geometry

In this chapter we will cover the routines in the `scipy.spatial` module that deal with the construction of triangulations of points in spaces of any dimension, and the corresponding convex hulls. The procedure is simple; given a set of *m* points in the *n*-dimensional space (which we represent as an *m x n* NumPy array), we create the `scipy.spatial` class `Delaunay`, containing the triangulation formed by those points.

```
>>> data = scipy.stats.randint.rvs(0.4,10,size=(10,2))
>>> triangulation = scipy.spatial.Delaunay(data)
```

Any `Delaunay` class has the basic search attributes such as `points` (to obtain the set of points in the triangulation), `vertices` (that offers the indices of vertices forming simplices in the triangulation), `neighbors` (for the indices of neighbor simplices for each simplex—with the convention that "-1" indicates no neighbor for simplices at the boundary).

More advanced attributes, for example `convex_hull`, indicate the indices of the vertices that form the convex hull of the given points. If we desire to search for the simplices that share a given vertex, we may do so with the `vertex_to_simplex` method. If, instead, we desire to locate the simplices that contain any given point in the space, we do so with the `find_simplex` method.

At this stage we would like to point out the intimate relationship between triangulations and Voronoi diagrams, and offer a simple coding exercise. Let us start by choosing first a random set of points, and obtaining the corresponding triangulation.

```
>>> locations=scipy.stats.randint.rvs(0,511,size=(2,8))
>>> triangulation=scipy.spatial.Delaunay(locations.T)
```

We may use the `matplotlib.pyplot` routine `triplot` to obtain a graphical representation of this triangulation. We first need to obtain the set of computed simplices. `Delaunay` offers us this set, but by means of the indices of the vertices instead of their coordinates. We thus need to map these indices to actual points before feeding the set of simplices to the `triplot` routine:

```
>>>assign_vertex = lambda index: triangulation.points[index]
>>>triangle_set = map(assign_vertex, triangulation.vertices)
>>>matplotlib.pyplot.triplot(locations[1], locations[0], \
... triangles=triangle_set, color='r')
```

We will now obtain the edge map of the Voronoi diagram in a similar fashion as we did before, and plot it below the triangulation (since the former needs to be with either a `pcolormesh` or `imshow` command).

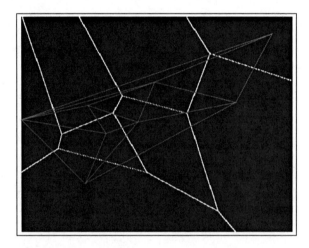

Note how the triangulation and the corresponding Voronoi diagrams are dual of each other; each edge in the triangulation (red) is perpendicular with an edge in the Voronoi diagram (white). How should we use this observation to code an actual Voronoi diagram for a cloud of points? The actual Voronoi diagram is the set of vertices and edges that composes it, rather than a binary image containing an approximation to the edges as we have computed.

Let us finish this chapter with two applications to scientific computing that use these techniques extensively, in combination with routines from other SciPy modules.

Structural model of oxides

In this example we will cover the extraction of the structural model of a molecule of a bronze-type Niobium oxide, from HAADF-STEM micrographs.

The following diagram shows HAADF-STEM micrograph of a bronze-type Niobium oxide (taken from `http://www.microscopy.ethz.ch/BFDF-STEM.htmhttp://www.microscopy.ethz.ch/BFDF-STEM.htm`, courtesy of ETH Zurich):

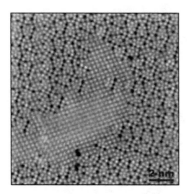

For pedagogical purposes, we took the following approach to solving this problem:

1. Segmentation of the atoms by thresholding and morphological operations.
2. Connected component labeling to extract each single atom for posterior examination.
3. Computation of the centers of mass of each label identified as an atom. This presents us with a lattice of points in the plane that shows a first insight in the structural model of the oxide.
4. Computation of the Voronoi diagram of the previous lattice of points. The combination of information with the output of the previous step will lead us to a decent (approximation of the actual) structural model of our sample.

Let us proceed in this direction.

Once retrieved, our HAADF-STEM images will be stored as big matrices with `float32` precision. For this project, it is enough to retrieve some tools from the `scipy.ndimage` module, and some procedures from the matplotlib library. The preamble then looks like the following code:

```
import numpy
import scipy
from scipy.ndimage import *
from scipy.misc import imfilter
import matplotlib.pyplot as plt
```

The image is loaded with the `imread(filename)` command. This stores the image as a `numpy.array` with `dtype = float32`. Notice that the maxima and minima are `1.0` and `0.0`, respectively. Other interesting information about the image can be retrieved:

```
img=imread('/Users/blanco/Desktop/NbW-STEM.png')
print "Image dtype: %s"%(img.dtype)
print "Image size: %6d"%(img.size)
print "Image shape: %3dx%3d"%(img.shape[0],img.shape[1])
print "Max value %1.2f at pixel %6d"%(img.max(),img.argmax())
print "Min value %1.2f at pixel %6d"%(img.min(),img.argmin())
print "Variance: %1.5f\nStandard deviation:
       %1.5f"%(img.var(),img.std())
```

This outputs the following information:

```
Image dtype: float32
Image size:  87025
Image shape: 295x295
Max value 1.00 at pixel  75440
Min value 0.00 at pixel   5703
Variance: 0.02580
Standard deviation: 0.16062
```

We perform thresholding by imposing an inequality in the array holding the data. The output is a Boolean array where `True` (white) indicates that the inequality is fulfilled, and `False` (black) otherwise. We may perform at this point several thresholding operations and visualize them to obtain the best threshold for segmentation purposes. The following images show several examples (different thresholdings applied to the oxide image):

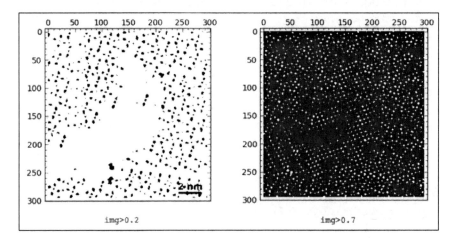

By visual inspection of several different thresholds, we choose `0.62` as one that gives us a good map showing what we need for segmentation. We need to get rid of "outliers", though; small particles that might fulfill the given threshold but are small enough not to be considered as an actual atom. Therefore, in the next step we perform a morphological operation of opening to get rid of those small particles. We decided that anything smaller than a square of size 2 x 2 is to be eliminated from the output of thresholding:

```
BWatoms = (img> 0.62)
BWatoms = binary_opening(BWatoms,structure=numpy.ones((2,2)))
```

We are ready for segmentation, which will be performed with the `label` routine from the `scipy.ndimage` module. It collects one slice per segmented atom, and offers the number of slices computed. We need to indicate the connectivity type. For example, in the following toy example, do we want to consider that situation as two atoms or one atom?

1	1	1	1	1	0
1	1	1	1	0	0
1	1	1	0	0	0
0	0	0	1	1	1
0	0	0	1	1	1
0	0	0	1	1	1

It depends; we would rather have it now as two different connected components, but for some other applications we might consider that they are one. The way we indicate the connectivity to the `label` routine is by means of a structuring element that defines feature connections. For example, if our criterion for connectivity between two pixels is that they are in adjacent edges, and then the structuring element looks like the image shown on the left-hand side from the images shown next. If our criterion for connectivity between two pixels is that they are also allowed to share a corner, then the structuring element looks like the image on the right-hand side. For each pixel we impose the chosen structuring element and count the intersections; if there are no intersections, then the two pixels are not connected. Otherwise, they belong to the same connected component.

0	1	0
1	1	1
0	1	0

1	1	1
1	1	1
1	1	1

We need to make sure that atoms that are too close in a diagonal direction are counted as two, rather than one, so we chose the structuring element on the left. The script then reads as follows:

```
structuring_element = [[0,1,0],[1,1,1],[0,1,0]]
segmentation,segments = label(BWatoms,structuring_element)
```

The `segmentation` object contains a list of slices, each of them with a Boolean matrix containing each of the found atoms of the oxide. We may obtain for each slice a great deal of useful information. For example, the coordinates of the centers of mass of each atom can be retrieved with the following commands:

```
coords  = center_of_mass(img, segmentation, range(1,segments+1))
xcoords = numpy.array([x[1] for x in coords])
ycoords = numpy.array([x[0] for x in coords])
```

Note that, because of the way matrices are stored in memory, there is a transposition of the x and y coordinates of the locations of the pixels. We need to take it into account.

Notice the overlap of the computed lattice of points over the original image (the left-hand side image from the two images shown next). We may obtain it with the following commands:

```
>>>plt.imshow(img); plt.gray(); plt.axis('off')
>>>plt.plot(xcoords,ycoords,'b.')
```

We have successfully found the centers of mass for most atoms, although there are still about a dozen regions where we are not too satisfied with the result. It is time to fine-tune by the simple method of changing the values of some variables; play with the threshold, with the structuring element, with different morphological operations, and so on. We can even add all the obtained information for a wide range of those variables, and filter out outliers. An example with optimized segmentation is shown, as follows (look at the right-hand side image):

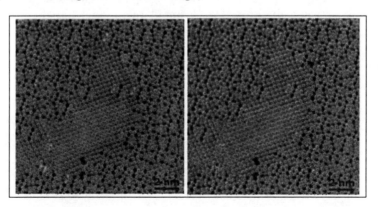

For the purposes of this exposition, we are happy to keep it simple and continue working with the set of coordinates that we have already computed. We will be now offering an approximation to the lattice of the oxide, computed as the edge map of the Voronoi diagram of the lattice.

```
L1,L2 = distance_transform_edt(segmentation==0,
return_distances=False,
return_indices=True)
Voronoi = segmentation[L1,L2]
Voronoi_edges= imfilter(Voronoi,'find_edges')
Voronoi_edges=(Voronoi_edges>0)
```

Let us overlay the result of `Voronoi_edges` with the locations of the found atoms:

```
>>>plt.imshow(Voronoi_edges); plt.axis('off'); plt.gray()
>>>plt.plot(xcoords,ycoords,'r.',markersize=2.0)
```

This gives the following output, which represents the structural model we were searching for:

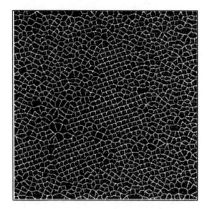

A finite element solver for Poisson's equation

We use finite elements when the size of the data is so large that it results prohibitive to deal with finite differences. To illustrate this case, we would like to explore the potential flow over a wing, as a solution to the Laplace equation subjects to certain boundary conditions.

We wish to create a simple profile of a wing, and produce a mesh surrounding it. This will be our starting point to solve this problem using finite elements, as we will be placing on the domain a piecewise continuous function, whose pieces are linear and supported on each of the triangles.

```
import numpy
from numpy import pi, cos, sin, hstack, vstack, linspace, where
from numpy import ones, multiply, cross, array, mat, zeros, mgrid
import scipy
import matplotlib.pyplot as plt
from scipy.special import exp10
from scipy.linalg import norm
from scipy.sparse import dok_matrix
from scipy.sparse.linalg import spsolve
from scipy.interpolate import LinearNDInterpolator
from scipy.spatial import Delaunay
```

We will be using two functions to generate vertices of our triangulation:

```
paramtr=lambda s:linspace(0,1,s)
ellipse=lambda a,b,s:[a*cos(2*pi*paramtr(s)), b*sin(2*pi*paramtr(s))]
```

We will start with a grid of a sufficiently large domain where the wing profile is to be included. We will complement this basic grid with enough points on the wing profile, which is designed as an ellipse:

```
vertices=ellipse(128,16,48)
for k in range(16):
    vertices=hstack((vertices,ellipse(128+16*k,16+16*k,48+2*k)))
```

We will be restricting the domain to a small rectangular region. We wish to introduce enough points in that border:

```
horizontal=linspace(-200,200,26)
vertical=linspace(-100,100,16)
vertices=hstack((vertices,vstack((horizontal,100*ones(26)))))
vertices=hstack((vertices,vstack((horizontal,-100*ones(26)))))
vertices=hstack((vertices,vstack((-200*ones(16),vertical))))
vertices=hstack((vertices,vstack((200*ones(16),vertical))))
```

Let us now perform the restriction of vertices, as follows:

```
inside_vertices=where( multiply(abs(vertices[0])<=200,
    abs(vertices[1])<=100 ))
vertices=vertices[:,inside_vertices[0]]
```

We may create now the triangulation, and erase from it all triangles that are inside of the wing profile, and outside the rectangle `[-200,200]` x `[-100,100]`. We do so by computing the center of mass for each triangle, and discarding those triangles whose centers are inside of the ellipse, or outside the rectangle:

```
triangulation = Delaunay(vertices.T)
index2point = lambda index: triangulation.points[index]
```

```
all_centers = index2point(triangulation.vertices).mean(axis=1)
not_in_wing = lambda pt: (pt[0]/128)**2+(pt[1]/16)**2>=1
trngl_set=triangulation.vertices[where(map(not_in_wing,all_centers))]
```

We then have the following triangulation:

```
>>>plt.triplot(vertices[0],vertices[1],triangles=trngl_set)
```

This produces the following graph:

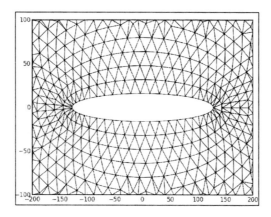

In this case, the flow potential is the solution of the Laplace equation, with boundary conditions as follows:

$$\begin{cases} -\Delta f = 0 \\ n \cdot \nabla f = 1 & \text{on } C_{\text{in}} \\ f = 0 & \text{on } C_{\text{out}} \\ n \cdot \nabla f = 0 & \text{elsewhere} \end{cases}$$

Here, C^{in} is the set of vertical edges on the leftmost side of the rectangle. C^{out} is the set of vertical edges on the rightmost side of the rectangle. We code the solution in the usual fashion. We compute the stiff matrix A (which for obvious reasons need to be sparse), the matrix R and the vector r holding the Robin conditions. With them, the solution to the system comes from the solution X of the system (A + R) X = r. This should be no trouble for SciPy. Let us start with the stiff matrix:

```
points=triangulation.points.shape[0]
stiff_matrix=dok_matrix((points,points))
Robin_matrix=dok_matrix((points,points))
Robin_vector=zeros((points,1))

for triangle in triangulation.vertices:
helper_matrix=dok_matrix((points,points))
```

```
        pt1,pt2,pt3=index2point(triangle)
        area=abs(0.5*cross(pt2-pt1,pt3-pt1))
        coeffs=0.5*vstack((pt2-pt3;pt3-pt1;pt1-pt2))/area
        helper_matrix[triangle,triangle]=array(mat(coeffs)*mat(coeffs).T)
    stiff_matrix=stiff_matrix+helper_matrix
```

Note the cumbersome way to update the matrix `stiff_matrix`. This is due to the fact that the matrix is sparse, and the current choice of representation does not behave well with indexing.

To compute the Robin matrix and vector we need to collect all edges on the boundary first. We also need to define the `kappa` and `gN` functions to help us design the boundary conditions:

```
kappa=lambda pt: exp10(6)*(pt[0]>99.99)
gN=lambda pt:float(pt[0]<=99.99)


for edge in triangulation.convex_hull:
helper_matrix=dok_matrix((points,points))
    length=norm(index2point(edge))
    center=mean(index2point(edge),axis=0)
helper_matrix[edge,edge]= length*kappa(center)*array([2,1,1,2])
Robin_matrix=Robin_matrix+helper_matrix
Robin_vector[edge]+=gN(center)*length*0.5*ones((2,1))
```

We are ready to solve the equation, precisely by computing the linear interpolant on the vertices of the triangulation, with the values obtained in our previous step:

```
>>>sltn_v=spsolve(stiff_matrix+Robin_matrix,Robin_vector)
>>> solution=LinearNDInterpolator(triangulation.points,sltn_v)
>>>X,Y=mgrid[-200:200,-100:100]
>>>plt.imshow(solution(-X,Y).T)
```

This produces the following image showing velocity potential for the wing profile:

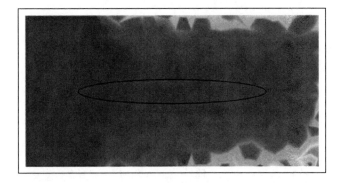

Summary

In the previous five chapters we have covered at length all the different modules included in the SciPy libraries, in a structured manner derived from the logical division of the different branches of mathematics.

We have also witnessed the power of this system to accomplish with minimal coding and optimal resource use, state-of-the-art applications to research problems in different areas of science.

In the next chapter we will introduce one of the main strengths of SciPy – the ability to interact with other languages.

8
Interaction with Other Languages

We often need to incorporate into our workflow some code written in different languages; mostly C/C++ or Fortran, and also from R, Matlab, or Octave. Python excels at allowing code from all these other sources to run from within; care must be taken to convert different numerical types to something that Python understands, but this is pretty much the only issue we encounter.

Fortran

SciPy provides a simple way of including Fortran code – f2py. This is a utility shipped with the NumPy libraries, which is operative when distutils from SciPy are available. This is always the case when we install SciPy.

The f2py utility is supposed to run outside of Python, and it is used to create from any Fortran file, a Python module that can be easily called in our sessions. Under any *nix system, we call it from the terminal. Under Windows, we recommend to run it in the native terminal, or even better, through a cygwin session.

Before being compiled with f2py, any Fortran code needs to undergo three basic changes, as follows:

- Removal of all allocations
- Transformation of the whole program into a subroutine
- If anything special needs to be passed to f2py, we must add it with the comment string "!f2py" or "cf2py"

Let us illustrate the process with a simple example. The following naïve subroutine, which we store in the `primefactors.f` file, performs a factorization in prime numbers for any given integer:

```
SUBROUTINE PRIMEFACTORS(num, factors, f)
  IMPLICIT NONE
  INTEGER, INTENT(IN) :: num    !input number
  INTEGER,INTENT(OUT), DIMENSION((num/2))::factors
  INTEGER, INTENT(INOUT) :: f
  INTEGER :: i, n
  i = 2
  f = 1
  n = num
  DO
    IF (MOD(n,i) == 0) THEN
      factors(f) = i
      f = f+1
      n = n/i
    ELSE
      i = i+1
    END IF
    IF (n == 1) THEN
      f = f-1
      EXIT
    END IF
  END DO
END SUBRO
UTINE PRIMEFACTORS
```

Since no allocation was made in the code, and we receive a subroutine directly, we may skip to the third step, but for the moment we will not tamper with f2py commands, and are content with trying to create a python module from it. The fastest way to wrap this `primefactors` subroutine is by issuing the following command:

```
% f2py -c primefactors.f -m primefactors
```

If everything is correct, an extension module with the name `primefactors.so` is created. We can then access the `primefactors` routine in Python from the `primefactors` module:

```
>>> import primefactors
>>>primefactors.primefactors(6,1)
array([2, 3, 0], dtype=int32)
```

C/C++

Technically, f2py can also wrap C code for us, but there are more efficient ways to perform this task. For instance, if we need to interface a very large library of C functions, the preferred method is **Simplified Wrapper and Interface Generator (SWIG)**. To wrap C++ code, depending on features required and the method of interacting with Python, we have several methods such as SWIG or f2py again, but also PyCXX, Boost.Python, or the SciPy module, weave. When C compilers are not available (and thus linking extensive libraries is not possible in the usual way), we use ctypes. Whenever we are going to use NumPy/SciPy code, and we seek fast solutions to our wrapping/binding, the most two common ways to interact with C/C++ are usually through the Python/C API, or through the weave package.

All the methods briefly enumerated here would require an entire monograph to describe at length the methodology of binding the nuisances of the wrapping depending on systems and requirements, and the caveats of their implementations. The method we would like to cover with more detail in this appendix is the weave package, more concretely by means of the inline routine. This command receives a string (raw or otherwise) containing a sequence of commands, and runs it in Python by calling your C/C++ compiler. The syntax is as follows:

```
inline(code, arg_names, local_dict=None, global_dict=None,
          force = 0,
          compiler='',
          verbose = 0,
support_code = None,
          customize=None,
type_factories = None,
auto_downcast=1,
          **kw)
```

Let us go over the different parameters:

- code is the string that holds the code to be run. Note that this code must not specify any kind of return statement. Instead, it should assign some result that can be returned to Python.

- The arg_names parameter is a list of strings containing the Python variable names that are to be sent to the C/C++ code.

- The local_dict parameter is optional, and must be a Python dictionary containing the values used as local scope for the C/C++ code.

- The global_dict parameter is also optional, and must be another Python dictionary containing the values that should be used as the global scope for the C/C++ code.

- The `force` parameter is used only for debugging purposes. It is also optional, and can take only two values – 0 (by default) or 1. If its value is set to 1, the C/C++ code is compiled every time inline is called.

- We may specify the compiler that takes over the C/C++ code with the `compiler` option. It must be a string containing the name of the C/C++ compiler.

For example, we could use the following method to employ `cout` for text displaying purposes:

```
>>> name = 'Francisco'
>>> pin = 1234
>>> code = 'std::code << name << "---PIN: " '
>>> code+= '<<std::hex << pin <<std::endl;'
>>>arg_names = ['name','pin']
>>> inline(code, arg_names)
Francisco---PIN: 4d2
```

That was a very simple example, in which no external header declarations were needed. If we wish to do so, those go in the `support_code` option. For instance, if we wish to include math functions from R in our C/C++ code, and pass it with inline, we need to perform the following steps:

1. Configure the C functions as a shared library. In the folder holding the R release, in a terminal session, issue the following command:

   ```
   % ./configure --enable-R-static-lib --enable-static --with-readline=no
   ```

2. Change to the folder `src/nmath/standalone` and finish the installation of libraries. At the end, we should have a file named `libRmath.so`, which needs to be pointed to from the `libpath` string back in our Python session:

   ```
   % cd src/nmath/standalone
   % make
   ```

3. Back in our Python session, we prepare the inline call with the proper options. For instance, if we wish to call the R routine `pbinom`, we proceed as follows:

   ```
   >>>support_code= 'extern "C" double pbinom(double x,\
   ... double n, double p, intlower_tail, intlog_p);'
   >>>library_dirs=[libpath]
   >>> libraries=['Rmath']
   ```

```
>>>runtime_library_dirs=[libpath]
>>> code='return_val=pbinom(100,20000,100./20000.,0,1);'
>>> inline(code, support_code, library_dirs, libraries,\
... runtime_library_dirs)
-0.7477349
```

Note how the function declaration is passed in `support_code`, not in code. Also, note that this option needs to start with `extern "C"` whenever we are not using C++.

4. If extra headers need to be passed, we do so with the `header` option, rather than `support_code` or `code`:

```
>>> headers = ['<math.h>']
```

We have a word of advice. Care must be taken while converting the different variable types from their original C/C++ format to something that Python understands. This requires modifying the original C/C++ code in certain cases. But by default, we do not have to worry about the following C/C++ types, as SciPy automatically turns them into the indicated Python formats, as shown in the following table:

Python	int	float	complex	string	list	dict	tuple
C/C++	int	double	std:: complex	py:: string	py:: list	py: dict	py:: tuple

File types `FILE*` are sent to Python files. Python callables and instances are both obtained from `py::object`. NumPy ndarrays are constructed from `PyArrayObject*`. For any other Python type to be used, the corresponding C/C++ types must be carefully turned into combinations of the previous.

And that should be all. To go beyond trivial uses of the inline function, we usually create extension modules and catalog the functions within for future use.

Matlab/Octave

Since both numerical computing environments provide with a fourth-generation programming language, we discourage the straightforward inclusion of code from any of these two. There is no gain in terms of speed, resource usage, or coding power. In the extreme and rare cases in which a specific routine is not available in SciPy, the preferred way to bring it to our session is by generating C code from the Matlab/Octave code, and then wrap it with any of the methods suggested in the previous section.

There is a different story when we receive data created from within Matlab or Octave. SciPy has a dedicated module to deal with this situation – `scipy.io`.

Let us show by example. We start in Octave, where we generate a Delaunay triangulation of a random set of 10 points in the plane. We save the coordinates of these points, as well as the pointers to the triangles in the triangulation, to a Matlab-style file (version 7) called `data`.

```
octave:1> x=rand(1,10);

octave:2> y=rand(size(x));

octave:3> T=Delaunay(x,y);

octave:4> save -v7 data x y T
```

We are done there. We go to our Python session, where we recover the file data.

```
>>> from scipy.io import loadmat

>>> datadict = loadmat("data")
```

The `datadict` variable holds a Python dictionary, with the names of the variables as keys, and the loaded matrices as their corresponding values:

```
>>>datadict.keys()

['__header__', '__globals__', 'T', 'y', 'x', '__version__']

>>>datadict['x']

array([[0.81222999,0.51836246,0.60425982,0.23660352,0.01305779,

        0.0875166,0.77873049,0.70505801,0.51406693,0.65760987]])

>>>datadict['__header__']

'MATLAB 5.0 MAT-file, written by Octave 3.2.4, 2012-11-27

 15:45:20 UTC'
```

It is possible to save data from our sessions to a format that Matlab and Octave will understand. We do so with the `savemat` command, from the same module. The syntax is as follows:

```
savemat(file_name, mdict, appendmat=True, format='5',
long_field_names=False, do_compression=False,
oned_as=None)
```

The `file_name` parameter contains the name of the Matlab-type file where the data will be written. The Python dictionary `mdict` contains the names (as keys) of the variables, and their corresponding array values.

If we wish to append `.mat` at the end of the file, we may do so in the `file_name` variable, or setting `appendmat` to `True`. In case we need to provide long names for the files (which not all versions of Matlab accept), we need to indicate so by setting the `long_field_names` option to `True`.

We may indicate the version of Matlab with the `format` option. We set it to the string `'5'` for versions 5 and later, or to the string `'4'` for version 4.

It is possible to compress the matrices we send, and we indicate so by setting the `do_compression` option to `True`.

The last option is very interesting. It allows us to indicate Matlab/Octave whether our arrays are to be read column by column, or row by row. Setting the `oned_as` parameter to the string `'column'` will send our data into a collection of column vectors. If we set it to the string `'row'`, it will send the data as collections of row vectors. If set to `None`, the format in which the data was written is respected.

Summary

This chapter introduced one of the main strengths of SciPy – the ability to interact with other languages such as C/C++, Fortran, R, and MATLAB®/Octave.

Index

Symbols

-diff (for derivative/integral) 83
-fft 82

A

adaptive quadrature 74
affine_transform command 90
Airy function 58, 59
arange command 30
arg_names parameter 125
array object 24, 25
array routines 26
audio.wav command 85
average/UPGMA method 107

B

Bairy function 58, 59
banana function 54
BarycentricInterpolator 62
Bessel functions 59, 60
beta integrals 74
BFGS algorithm 68
Biggles
  URL 8
block diagonal matrices 43
Brent method 69
Brent method for scalar function 68
bronze-type Niobium oxide
  HAADF-STEM micrograph 113
brute force 68

C

C/C++
  about 7, 125
  arg_names parameter 125
  code parameter 125
  compiler option 126
  data 128
  force parameter 126
  global_dict parameter 125
  header option 127
  local_dict parameter 125
  support_code option 126
center_of_mass command 95
centroid/UPGMC method 107
Chaco
  URL 8
Chebyshev polynomials 56
chirp 84
Chi-square test (chisquare) 98
Cholesky decomposition 48
Cin 119
circulant matrices 43
clustering
  about 105
  hierarchical clustering 107-110
  vector quantization and k-means 105-107
clustering mammals
  downloading, URL 109
COBYLA 68
code parameter 125
companion matrices 43
compiler option 126
complete/max/farthest method 107

composite trapezoidal rule 74
computational geometry 111
compute item frequencies (itemfreq) 96
constrained minimization 68
contourf command 58
convenience functions 53, 54
convex_hull 111
Cophenetic distances between observations
        (cophenet) 108
Cout 119
crude bisection method 69
cumulative and relative frequencies (cum-
        freq, relfreq) 96
cumulative distribution function (cdf) 96
curve_fit routine 68
cval option 91
cval parameter 87

D

data 128
datadict variable 128
data mining
    about 95
    clustering 105
    distances 101, 102
    statistics 95, 96
datatype 21, 22
Dawson's integral 72
Delaunay class 111
DFT 81-83
dir() command 13
Discrete Fourier Transforms. *See* DFT
distances
    about 101, 102
    first warning 102
    fourth warning 104, 105
    second warning 103
    third warning 103
distributions
    about 96, 97
    fitting 100, 101
distutils 123
do_compression option 129
documentation
    finding 13-15
downhill simplex algorithm 68

E

Eigenvalue issues 47
elliptic functions 60
elliptic integrals 73
exponential integrals 72

F

f2py utility 123
fft2 82
fftn 82
fig.show() command 17
file argument 84
file_name parameter 128
filters
    about 85, 86
    creating 85
    design 88
    image interpolation 90-92
    LTI system theory 88
    morphology 92, 93
    window functions 88, 89
find_simplex method 111
finite elements
    for Poissons equation 117-120
Finite impulse response (FIR) 88
fixed-order Gaussian quadrature 74
fixed-tolerance Gaussian quadrature 74
fname argument 85
force parameter 126
format option 129
Fortran 7, 123, 124

G

gamma function 56, 57
gamma integrals 74
Gauss error functions 72
gausspulse 83, 84
Gegenbauer polynomials 56
geometric_transform routine 90
Git repositories 9
global_dict parameter 125
GNU Octave system 6
Golden method for scalar function 68

H

HAADF-STEM micrograph
of bronze-type Niobium oxide 113
Hadamard matrices 43
Hankel functions 60
Hankel matrices 43
header option 127
Hermite polynomials 56
Hessenberg decompositions 48
Hessian matrix 54
hierarchical clustering
about 107
average/UPGMA method 107
centroid/UPGMC method 107
complete/max/farthest method 107
Cophenetic distances between observations
(cophenet) 108
inconsistency statistics (inconsistent) 108
maximum inconsistency coefficient for
each non-singleton cluster with its
descendants (maxdists) 108
maximum statistic for each non-singleton
cluster with its descendants (maxRstat)
108
median/WPGMC method 107
ndarray 108
pdist routine 108
single/min/nearest method 107
Ward's linkage method 107
weighted/WPGMA method 107
hilbert 83
Hilbert matrices 43
HippoDraw
URL 8
histograms (histogram, histogram2) 96
Horner schemes 53
hyperbolic trigonometric integrals 73
hypergeometric functions 60

I

ifft2 (two dimensions) 82
ifftn (any number of dimensions) 82
ifft (one dimension) 82
ifftshift 82
ihilbert (for the Hilbert transform) 83

image compression
via singular value decomposition 48, 49
image interpolation 90
imread(filename) command 114
imshow command 112
inconsistency statistics (inconsistent) 108
indexing 22, 23
Infinite impulse response (IIR) 88
installation, SciPy 8-10
integration
about 72
beta integrals 74
elliptic integrals 73
exponential integrals 72
gamma integrals 74
hyperbolic trigonometric integrals 73
logarithm integrals 72
numerical integration 74
trigonometric integrals 73
interpolation 60-64
interval estimation 97
inverse Hilbert matrices 43
iOS 8
iPad 8
itilbert (for the h-Tilbert transform
of periodic sequences) 83

J

Jacobi polynomials 56

K

Kelvin functions 60
Kendall's tau for ordinal data
(kendalltau) 97
k-means technique 105, 106
Kolmogorov-Smirnov tests 98
KrogInterpolator command 62

L

label command 95
label routine 115
Lagrange interpolation 61
Laguerre polynomials 56
L-BFGS-S algorithm 68
least-squares algorithm 68

Legendre ploynomials 56
Leslie matrices 43
linregress routine 97
linspace command 30
log1p function 54
logarithm integrals 72
logspace command 30
Lorenz attractors 77, 79
lower-triangular matrices 43
lti class 88
LTI system theory 88
lu command 47
lufactor command 47

M

macports 9
Maple® 6, 7
mat command 39
Mathematica® 6, 7
Mathieu functions 60
Matlab 127
MATLAB® 6, 7
matplotlib.pyplot routine 112
matrix
  about 39
  creating 39-43
  functions 45, 46
  operations 44
matrix command 39
matrix decompositions 47
matrix methods
  about 44
  Eigenvalue problems 47
  functions, on matrices 45, 46
  image compression, via singular value
      decomposition (SVD) 48, 49
  matrix decompositions 47
  operations, between matrices 44
  solvers 49, 50
matrix structure 39
maximum inconsistency coefficient for each
      non-singleton cluster with its de-
      scendants (maxdists) 108
maximum statistic for each non-single-
      ton cluster with its descendants
      (maxRstat) 108

MayaVi for 3D rendering
  URL 8
medfilt 85
median/WPGMC method 107
minimization 68
mode option 91
morphology
  operations 92, 93

N

ndarray 83, 108
n-dimensional space 111
neighbors 111
Newton-Raphson method 69
nonlinear conjugate gradient 68
numerical integration 74
NumPy 5, 7
NumPy ndarrays 127
numpy.putmask() command 29
numpy.where() command 29

O

object 20, 21
Octave 127-129
oned_as parameter 129
optimal weightings
  example 43
optimization
  about 68
  minimization 68
  roots 69, 72
order parameter 91
ordinary differential equations 75, 77
orthonormal bases
  example 44
overwrite_x 82
oxides
  structural mode 113, 115
  structural model 113-116

P

Palm OS 8
parabolic cylinder functions 60
PCHIP monotonic cubic interpolation 63

pcolormesh command 112
pdist routine 108
Pearson correlation coefficient (pearsonr) 97
PIL 8
Pivoted LU decomposition 47
PlayStation
  about 8
point biserial correlation (pointbiserialr) 97
Poissons equation
  finite elements 117-120
polyfit command 65
Powell's method 68
primefactors.f file 124
primefactors routine 124
primefactors subroutine 124
probability density function (pdf) 96
programming environment, for
      computational mathematics
  characteristics 5, 6
Psion 8
PSP 8
Python
  about 7
  URL 8
Python 2 8
Python 3 8
Python Imaging Library (PIL) 85
PythonMath 8

Q

QR decompositions 48
quadrature formulae 74
QZ decompositions 48

R

random variable per se (rvs) 96
regression 65, 66
Riccati-Bessel functions 60
Ridders' algorithm 69
Riemann zeta function 57
Robin matrix 120
Romberg integration 74
roots 69-72
Rosenbrock function 69
routines
  for array creation 26-31

for array manipulation 34, 35
for combination of multiple arrays 32, 33
for extracting information, from arrays 35,
      36
RPy 8
rv_continuous class 96
rv_discrete class 96

S

Sage 7
Sage Math 8
sawtooth 83, 84
Schur decompositions 48
scientific visualization 16
Scilab® 6
SciPy
  about 5, 7, 81
  documentation, finding 13-15
  installing 8-10
  integration method 72
  interpolation method 60-64
  optimization 68
  modules 10
  ordinary differential equations 75-77
  regression method 65, 66
  scientific visualization 16
  special functions, evaluating 53
  URL 9
scipy.cluster 10, 95
scipy.cluster.hierachy submodule 108
scipy.cluster.vq (vector quantization) 95
scipy.constants 10
scipy.fftpack module 10, 82, 83
SciPy, for linear algebra
  matrix, creating 39-43
  matrix methods 44
scipy.integrate module 10, 53, 72
scipy.integrate.quad_explain() command 74
scipy.interpolate 10
scipy.interpolate module 53, 60
scipy.io 10
scipy.lib 10
scipy.linalg module 10, 43-45
scipy.misc.lena 20
scipy.misc library 20
scipy.misc module 10, 84

scipy.ndimage.measurements 95
scipy.ndimage.measurements
    submodule 95
scipy.ndimage module
  about 85, 86, 115
  creating 81
scipy.optimize module 10, 53, 69
SciPy organization 10-12
scipy.signal module 10, 85-88
scipy.sparse module 10, 40, 43
scipy.spatial module 10, 95, 111
scipy.special module 10, 53, 56, 57, 69, 72
scipy.stats.kde submodule 101
scipy.stats module 10, 95, 96
scipy.weave 10
segmentation object 116
sequential least-squares programming 68
set_integrator method 75
signal construction 83-85
signal processing 81
signal-to-noise ratio (signaltonoise) 96
Simplified Wrapper and Interface Generator
    (SWIG) 125
Simpson's rule 74
simulated annealing 68
single/min/nearest method 107
singular value decomposition 47
singular value decomposition (SVD) 48
solvers 49, 50
sourceforge 9
Spearman's rank-order correlation
    (spearmanr) 97
special functions evaluation, Scipy
  about 53
  Airy function 58, 59
  Bairy function 58, 59
  Bessel functions 59, 60
  convenience functions 53, 54
  gamma function 56, 57
  Riemann zeta function 57
  Struve functions 59, 60
  test functions 53, 54
  univariate polynomials 54-56
Spence's dilogarithm 72
spheroidal wave functions 60
square 83, 84

square Pascal matrices 43
standard error (sem) 96
statistics
  about 95
  correlation measures 97
  distribution fitting 100, 101
  distributions 96
  interval estimation 97
  statistical tests 98, 99
Struve functions 59, 60
support_code option 126
survival function along with its inverse
    (sf, isf) 96
svd command 47
System for Algebra and Geometry
    Experimentation. *See* Sage

T

test functions 53, 54
tilbert 83
todense method 41
Toeplitz matrices 43
trigonometric functions 53
trigonometric integrals 73
triplot 112
triplot routine 112
truncated Newton's algorithm 68

U

univariate polynomials 54-56

V

vector 120
vector quantization 105-107
vertex_to_simplex method 111
vertices 111
Voronoi diagram 112
Voronoi_edges 117

W

wavfile submodule 85
weighted/WPGMA method 107
window functions 89

Thank you for buying
Learning SciPy for Numerical &
Scientific Computing

About Packt Publishing

Packt, pronounced 'packed', published its first book "*Mastering phpMyAdmin for Effective MySQL Management*" in April 2004 and subsequently continued to specialize in publishing highly focused books on specific technologies and solutions.

Our books and publications share the experiences of your fellow IT professionals in adapting and customizing today's systems, applications, and frameworks. Our solution based books give you the knowledge and power to customize the software and technologies you're using to get the job done. Packt books are more specific and less general than the IT books you have seen in the past. Our unique business model allows us to bring you more focused information, giving you more of what you need to know, and less of what you don't.

Packt is a modern, yet unique publishing company, which focuses on producing quality, cutting-edge books for communities of developers, administrators, and newbies alike. For more information, please visit our website: www.packtpub.com.

About Packt Open Source

In 2010, Packt launched two new brands, Packt Open Source and Packt Enterprise, in order to continue its focus on specialization. This book is part of the Packt Open Source brand, home to books published on software built around Open Source licences, and offering information to anybody from advanced developers to budding web designers. The Open Source brand also runs Packt's Open Source Royalty Scheme, by which Packt gives a royalty to each Open Source project about whose software a book is sold.

Writing for Packt

We welcome all inquiries from people who are interested in authoring. Book proposals should be sent to author@packtpub.com. If your book idea is still at an early stage and you would like to discuss it first before writing a formal book proposal, contact us; one of our commissioning editors will get in touch with you.

We're not just looking for published authors; if you have strong technical skills but no writing experience, our experienced editors can help you develop a writing career, or simply get some additional reward for your expertise.

NumPy 1.5 Beginner's Guide

ISBN: 978-1-84951-530-6   Paperback: 234 pages

An acti on-packed guide for the easy-to-use, high performance, Python based free open source NumPy mathemati cal library using real-world examples

1. The first and only book that truly explores NumPy practically

2. Perform high performance calculations with clean and efficient NumPy code

3. Analyze large data sets with statistical functions

4. Execute complex linear algebra and mathematical computations

NumPy Cookbook

ISBN: 978-1-84951-892-5   Paperback: 226 pages

Over 70 interesting recipes for learning the Python open source mathematical library, NumPy

1. Do high performance calculations with clean and efficient NumPy code

2. Analyze large sets of data with statistical functions

3. Execute complex linear algebra and mathematical computations

Please check **www.PacktPub.com** for information on our titles

Learning RStudio for R Statistical Computing

ISBN: 978-1-78216-060-1   Paperback: 126 pages

Learn to effectively perform R development, statistical analysis, and reporting with the most popular R IDE

1. A complete practical tutorial for RStudio, designed keeping in mind the needs of analysts and R developers alike

2. Step-by-step examples that apply the principles of reproducible research and good programming practices to R projects

3. Learn to effectively generate reports, create graphics, and perform analysis, and even build R-packages with RStudio

Python 3 Web Development Beginner's Guide

ISBN: 978-1-84951-374-6   Paperback: 336 pages

Use Python to create, theme, and deploy unique web applicati ons

1. Build your own Python web applications from scratch

2. Follow the examples to create a number of different Python-based web applications, including a task list, book database, and wiki application

3. Have the freedom to make your site your own without having to learn another framework

Please check **www.PacktPub.com** for information on our titles

0,80

CPSIA information can be obtained at www.ICGtesting.com
Printed in the USA
LVOW11s1555090414

381020LV00009B/602/P